Phillis Wheatley as Prophetic Poet

Rhetoric, Race, and Religion

Series Editor: Andre E. Johnson, University of Memphis

This series will provide space for emerging, junior, or senior scholars engaged in research that studies rhetoric from a race or religion perspective. This will include studies contributing to our understanding of how rhetoric helps shape race and/or religion and how race and/or religion shapes rhetoric. In this series, scholars seek to examine phenomena from either a historical or contemporary perspective. Moreover, we are interested in how race and religion discourse function rhetorically.

Recent Titles in This Series

Phillis Wheatley as Prophetic Poet: You Must Be Born Again by Wallis C. Baxter III

Reverend Albert Cleage Jr. and the Black Prophetic Tradition: A Reintroduction of The Black Messiah by Earle J. Fisher

Rhetorics of Race and Religion on the Christian Right: Barack Obama and the War on Terror by Samuel P. Perry

Rhetoric, Race, Religion, and the Charleston Shootings: Was Blind but Now I See by Sean Patrick O'Rourke and Melody Lehn

Rhetoric and the Responsibility to and for Language: Speaking of Evil by Matthew Boedy

The Struggle over Black Lives Matter and AllLivesMatter by Amanda Nell Edgar and Andre E. Johnson

Desegregation and the Rhetorical Fight for African American Citizenship Rights by Sally F. Paulson

Contemporary Christian Culture: Messages, Missions, and Dilemmas edited by Omotayo Banjo Adesagba and Kesha Morant Williams

The Motif of Hope in African American Preaching during Slavery and the Post-Civil War Era: There's a Bright Side Somewhere by Wayne E. Croft

The Womanist Preacher: Proclaiming Womanist Rhetoric from the Pulpit by Kimberly P. Johnson

Phillis Wheatley as Prophetic Poet

You Must Be Born Again

Wallis C. Baxter III

LEXINGTON BOOKS
Lanham • Boulder • New York • London

Published by Lexington Books
An imprint of The Rowman & Littlefield Publishing Group, Inc.
4501 Forbes Boulevard, Suite 200, Lanham, Maryland 20706
www.rowman.com

86-90 Paul Street, London EC2A 4NE

Copyright © 2022 by The Rowman & Littlefield Publishing Group, Inc.

"Harlem [2]" from THE COLLECTED POEMS OF LANGSTON HUGHES by Langston Hughes, edited by Arnold Rampersad with David Roessel, Associate Editor, copyright © 1994 by the Estate of Langston Hughes. Used by permission of Alfred A. Knopf, an imprint of the KnopfDoubleday Publishing Group, a division of Penguin Random House LLC. All rights reserved.
R. Lynn Matson. Phillis Wheatley - Soul Sister. ©1972 Phylon.

All rights reserved. No part of this book may be reproduced in any form or by any electronic or mechanical means, including information storage and retrieval systems, without written permission from the publisher, except by a reviewer who may quote passages in a review.

British Library Cataloguing in Publication Information Available

Library of Congress Cataloging-in-Publication Data

Names: Baxter, Wallis C., III, author.
  Title: Phillis Wheatley as prophetic poet : you must be born again / Wallis C. Baxter III.
  Description: Lanham : Lexington Books, [2022] | Series: Rhetoric, race, and religion | Includes bibliographical references and index. | Summary: "In You Must Be Born Again: Phillis Wheatley as Prophetic Poet the author presents Phillis Wheatley as a preacher and theologian committed to transforming her world through her poetry. The result is a prophetic message of hope for the oppressed and corrective instruction for the institutional power structures"-- Provided by publisher.
  Identifiers: LCCN 2021053815 (print) | LCCN 2021053816 (ebook) | ISBN 9781793641205 (cloth) | ISBN 9781793641229 (pbk) | ISBN 9781793641212 (epub)
  Subjects: LCSH: Wheatley, Phillis, 1753-1784--Criticism and interpretation. | Wheatley, Phillis, 1753-1784--Religion. | Liberation theology in literature. | African Americans--Religious life. | Religious poetry, American--History and criticism. | American poetry--African American authors--History and criticism. | American poetry--Women authors--History and criticism. | Poetry, Modern--18th century--History and criticism. | African American women poets--Biography.
  Classification: LCC PS866.W5 Z565 2022 (print) | LCC PS866.W5 (ebook) | DDC 811/.1--dc23/eng/20211123
  LC record available at https://lccn.loc.gov/2021053815
  LC ebook record available at https://lccn.loc.gov/2021053816

In loving memory of Elease Hampton Baxter and to my son, Elijah, and every meaningful moment to come in his life. I pray you become the man God has designed you to be.

Contents

Acknowledgments	ix
Introduction	1
Chapter 1: Phillis Wheatley, the Poet-Theologian	17
Chapter 2: Encountering God through the Preacher: Wheatley's Influences	33
Chapter 3: The Spoken Word: On Isaiah 63:1–8	45
Chapter 4: Created in the Imagination	59
Chapter 5: Salvation Is Available	77
Chapter 6: The Story behind the Voice	107
Epilogue: To Whom Much is Given	117
Appendix 1	123
Bibliography	127
Index	133
About the Author	141

Acknowledgments

First and foremost, I have to thank my lord and savior Jesus Christ, who was born of a virgin birth, lived, served, healed, delivered, was crucified, dead and buried, yet lives and is head of my life. Without God in my life, I truly do not know where I would be. This entire project is God-breathed, not in the sense that this book is scripture but because I literally asked God to speak through me and to me as I sought to put pen to paper. I know without a shadow of a doubt that this project would not be what it is if I did not have God as the constant. When no one else was around, God remained the one constant. God encouraged me, pushed me, consoled me, and reminded me that I and this book project belonged to God. So, again I say thanks be unto God!

I would like to thank my academic village, past and present. I'll begin with Drs. Dana A. Williams and Albert Turner for their time, attention, and dedication to this project whether through meaningful conversation or otherwise. Your willingness to question, (re)direct, coach, encourage, challenge and guide me with regard to this project is appreciated. You each have in some way helped me fine-tune my voice. You constantly remind me of my potential and that there is always life to be lived and scholarship in which to engage. Now, to my big sister Dr. Williams, little did I know our journey would bring us here. Perhaps you knew. You consistently push me to maximize my potential as a scholar. I am forever grateful for the bond we have formed. You saw and see something in me that no one else saw/sees. I'm grateful you chose to struggle with me because (in the words of Douglass) the struggle has resulted in true progress. You're awesome! Thank you.

Dr. Albert Turner you have pushed me from day one on the campus of Morehouse College. You are the reason I was able to graduate on time! More than that, you have remained a constant intellectual sounding board in my life. I also think it helps that (as you say) you are a called preacher who is just in hiding. You are able to lend your inquisitive spirit, heart, and mind to give me insights into texts that are unique and, ultimately, transformational. My critical lens has been shaped in many ways by you.

To my Duke Divinity and University Family, thank you for all you did to help shape me theologically and socially. To the Div School faculty, past and present: Drs. J. Kameron Carter, Amy Laura Hall, C. Kavin Rowe, J. Warren Smith, Willie Jennings, Esther Acolaste, Curtis Freeman, and my advisor William Claire Turner, Jr. You helped me find my theological lens and voice. To the University faculty, past and present, Drs. Mark Anthony Neal (MAN), and Maurice O. Wallace. I cannot say enough about MAN and Maurice. MAN, you showed me that scholarship does not have to be detached from reality. You pushed me as my advisor within the certificate program to use my theological training to read social conditions and popular culture. Maurice, my big brother, confidante, friend, golfing buddy, you were the second example I encountered of an academician who was actively pastoring a church, but you were the first I encountered in my field. You are more than my example of a literary scholar who pastors, you are my inspiration to be the best I can be at both. I know we will continue to sojourn together!

The journey began in many ways at the greatest HBCU in all the land, Morehouse College. I was able to develop a love for African American literature and Black Theology in Brawley Hall, Sale Hall, and King Chapel. To my undergraduate advisor, Dr. Melvin Rahming, you told me early in my collegiate career that I had what it took to get a graduate degree in English. I am where I am now in large part due to your affirmation. Dean Lawrence Carter, you play a significant role in this as well because you are the one who told me that pursuing a graduate degree in English would help my preaching in ways I could not imagine . . . you were right. To Rev. Dr. Aaron L. Parker, you were the first example of a preacher-scholar for me. The way you are able to blend the best of the academy with the best of the church is simply amazing. You care for your students just as much as you care for your church members. You teach as passionately and in depth in bible study as you do in Systematic Theology, Introduction to Religion, or your class on Marcus Garvey. To each of you, thank you.

I cannot talk about Morehouse without talking about Spelman. To all my adopted "Spelman" family past and present, to Mrs. Candace Raven, Dr. Cynthia Spence, Dr. Akiba "Mama-Dean" Harper, Dean Desiree Pedescleaux, my big sis D-Kim, Dr. Anne Warner (thanks to you Harriet Jacobs will always be my chick on the side), my unofficial church member Tarshia Stanley, my intellectual pulse check partner Michelle Hite, my soul brother and writing accountability partner Richard Benson; I thank each and every one of you, for you have contributed to my formation in life and academia.

To my Georgetown family, Drs. Angelyn Mitchell and Robert Patterson, you each challenged me in different ways. Dr. Patterson, you push me scholarly in more ways than you know. My prayer is that I can be as impassioned with my scholarship as you are. Dr. Mitchell, you gave me an opportunity that no one else would at the time. That opportunity helped me hone my philosophy of teaching. I cannot express how significant that was to me.

To all of those who have read with me, written with me, read chapters for me, or just allowed me to dump my issues with the process on you, thank you. Thank you to Kendra and Tori, and all those I cannot think of at the moment.

At this point, I must thank those who are connected to me spiritually. To my Second Baptist family, thank you for allowing me to practice prophetic ministry with you. I am grateful to serve as your pastor and thankful for the freedom to be in both the church and the academy. I do not take that privilege for granted. To my God-brother Timothy J. Walker, and my Godfather Thomas L. Walker, thank you for your consistent encouragement, prayers, dialogue, and support through allowing me to preach in your pulpits. To my DMV crew, Pastors Kendrick Curry, D. Mitchell Ford, Bill Lamar, Lucius Dalton, Joseph Norman Evans, Courtenay Miller, President Lester McCorn, Bowyer Freeman, Steve Russell, Eric Barksdale, Eric Baldwin, Antoine Hutchins, Richard Holland, Keith William Byrd, Sr., and the rest thank you for your constant encouragement.

To my boys (in no particular order), Lyle Pointer, Marquez Ball, Justin Rhodes, Donald Cook, Lavee Sims, Hector Arocho, Leo Brown, Vandy Gaffney, and Ernest Brooks you have said something, done something, gone somewhere with me that has encouraged me, inspired me, challenged me, or just made me laugh. Thank you for the brotherhood!

Finally, and perhaps most importantly, I must thank my family. Shayla, you know how important you are to me. You have walked with me throughout this journey. We've prayed together, played together, cried together, laughed together, lived together, and are trying to raise a black boy in this crazy society. With you, I know it and more can be done. As I've said before, you are truly a God-send, and I look forward to seeing what God continues to do in your life and our life together.

To all those who have gone before me, Aunt Edith, Uncle Jimmy, Grandad Wallace, Grandma Elease, Grandma Queenie, Uncle Bub, and there are many, many more, I stand on each and every one of your shoulders. To my uncles, aunts, and cousins, I thank each of you. You have made this journey memorable and, at times, comical. I can't wait for the next family reunion. To my extended family, which seems to grow daily, you know who you are; you have made this journey a little bit easier. You are inspiring and an inspiration. I'm grateful to God to consider you family.

To Grandad Bubba, you have always been an inspiration to me. Though you never had the opportunity to get an education past grade school, you are an entrepreneur and businessman second to none. I salute you and hope one day I can maximize my potential like you. To John and June Aldridge, though I'm not your blood grandson, I never knew or felt it. You have been my example for what a successful life partnership looks like. Grandfather John, you are the quintessential Morehouse Man. I only hope to live up to your example. Grandmother June, you are the most stylish woman I know. Your style of course complements your intellect and passion for life. You were the first person I knew with a PhD in English, so in some way you are the reason I have gotten to this point.

Antheny "Amp" Hampton, you are my brother/uncle. I would not have it any other way. I love you and appreciate you more than you'll ever know. My prayer is that we both maximize our potential in all that we do. I know you believe in me, and, if I haven't said it before, I believe in you bro!

Dad, you kept asking questions, even when I didn't want to answer them. You proved by your actions more than anything else how much you love, support, appreciate, and trust me. I really don't have the words, but, man to man, I love you and hope that I can one day provide for my son the way you have for me. You are the greatest man I know—God-fearing, Family-loving, fun, energetic, intelligent, and consistent. I tip my hat to you sir!

Mom, you are the wind beneath my wings. Like our favorite book says, "I'll love you for always," and there is nothing you can do about it. Your honey pumpkin has been through ups and downs, and you have been there the entire journey. You pushed me when I didn't want to be pushed. You forced me to write when I thought I didn't have anything to say. You literally would've taken on all of the hardship, struggles, illnesses, surgeries and whatever else for me, and I want you to know, it is greatly appreciated. You are phenomenal, and my prayer is that I can be the encourager and source of strength for my son the way you have been for me. Thank you and praise God for you! I love you!

So, I end where I began. I am grateful to God!

Introduction

"I PLEAD THE FIRST!": WRITING A NEW AMERICA

Many consider James Cone to be the father of American liberation theology; I contend that Phillis Wheatley is its mother.[1] My rationale for this claim and approach to this investigation are both literary and theological. I must state at the outset that my theological convictions inform my literary critiques and intellectual journey. As I write these words, I am keenly aware of the dual nature of my personhood and approach to interrogation, having a sincere love for the academy and for the church. Both are significantly critical spaces and both foster nourishment, reform, and resistance (in multifaceted ways). For this reason, I try to identify the theological questions that undergird the line of literary inquiry. This arduous process is necessary to understanding the analysis herein, for I believe that the theological and literary do not exist in isolated vacuous spaces; rather, they are conversant and, in many ways, complementary. Since the focus is, in this instance, primarily literary and secondarily theological, I have provided a significant portion of the theological foundation in this introduction and the first chapter, "Phillis Wheatley, the Poet-Theologian."

Throughout the remaining chapters, the theological critique is subordinate to the literary critique, which informs the new ethic. For any and all biblical citations, I use the King James Version of the Bible because it is most likely the version that Phillis Wheatley and her contemporaries would have used. Margaret T. Hills and other noted scholars such as A. S. Herbert, Donald Brake, and S. L. Greenslade identify the King James Bible as the authoritative bible of the era rather than the Geneva Bible used by the Puritans during the colonial period; therefore, the King James Version was common in most households and would have been in the Wheatley's. In fact, William J. Scheick notes, Wheatley's exposure to Enlightenment thought and abolitionist theory most likely came from the pulpit of the New South Congregational Church.[2] He continues that by 1771, clergy . . . integrated religious and political concerns in their sermons. Also from the pulpit, as well as from her reading and her discussions with others, Wheatley became familiar with select standard eighteenth-century Protestant commentaries on Scripture and, as well with approved secular applications of biblical passages. Doubtless Wheatley was very attentive to these exegeses, for the King James version of the Bible was among a handful of her favorite books.[3]

Though there are more accurate translations in existence today (or at least more conceptually akin to the original Greek, Aramaic, and Hebrew languages and contexts), I have limited my interpretive scope to the resource to which Wheatley (and eighteenth-century America as well) would have had access to while attempting to biblically interpret the racial landscape of America. *You Must Be Born Again*, which will refer frequently to biblical texts, seeks to position Wheatley as an engaged examiner of her culture (her America) who recognizes the humanity of blacks and women while seeking to transform the cultural norms and subtly pursue equality for white and black people, which I suggest is a form of liberation theology. Wheatley, the poet, convincingly argues for an ethical rebirth in America.

Poetry is poetry. Abstract yet concrete, ethereal yet tangible, far-reaching yet grounded, poetry is representative of the human experience in powerful ways. Additionally, the poet can sagaciously demonstrate the liberation perspectives using techniques that are similar to preaching, an artistry which I examine succinctly in chapter 3, "The Spoken Word: On Isaiah 63:1–8." In this sense, Wheatley adds her voice to an extant chorus in eighteenth-century Americans seeking to engage the ever-evolving culture.

John Wheatley suggests that Phillis Wheatley's "own curiosity" led her to write. I contend that during the American Slavocracy, Phillis Wheatley writes to construct a perspective(s) of liberation with theological foundations countering the soteriological Eurocentric notions of divine election prevalent during the period and aimed at liberating an oppressed people socially, economically, and politically. Being born again is a complex and far-reaching concept for some and a critical and vital component of life for others. This project seeks to wed an enigmatic concept with an essential component for the sake of reclaiming (though some would argue that it first needs to be established) a unified/united understanding of and appreciation for all humanity. In the nineteenth century, the nation was starkly divided. In the early nineteenth century, the slavocracy proved a viable workforce, and black bodies were used for economic gain. In the mid-nineteenth century, Manifest Destiny propelled the expansion of ideas, ideals, and territory, inclusive of the proposition to extend the reach of chattel slavery. Amid political and ideological unrest, Abraham Lincoln signs the Emancipation Proclamation in 1863 "freeing" the enslaved. The trajectory of American civilization, it would seem, was on a unifying course. Yet, forty years later, at the turn of the century, black people were still underprivileged, and Reconstruction seemed to reconstitute, rebuild, and renew everything except race relations in America. For these reasons and upon the backdrop of this historical reality, many black writers prior to and during the nineteenth century argue for America "to be born again."

When I suggest that many black writers before and during the nineteenth century call for an American rebirth, I do not consider it solely in the Western ecclesiological notion of conversion and baptism. Neither do I consider it solely in the context of a West African river ritual of submersion and conversion. However, the transformative intent behind the act is apropos to the discussion, for the call to be born again is a call that reaches beyond the historical genesis of American culture as we know it to a time in antiquity—a different genesis. In the biblical creation account (and there are two), humankind is formed in the image and likeness of God.[4] At the end of the second creation account, however, God breathes the breath of life into humankind before a "living soul" can exist. According to mystic theologian Watchman Nee, the Bible does not merely relegate humankind to the two parts of body and soul. Rather,

> It treats man . . . as tripartite—spirit, soul and body.[5] [1 Thessalonians 5:23] shows that the whole man is divided into three parts. The Apostle Paul refers here to the complete sanctification of believers, "sanctify you wholly." According to the Apostle, how is a person wholly sanctified? By his spirit and soul and body being kept. From this we can easily understand that the whole person comprises these three parts. This verse also makes a distinction between spirit and soul; otherwise, Paul would have said simply "your soul." Since God has distinguished the human spirit from the human soul, we conclude that man is composed of not two, but three, parts: spirit, soul and body.[6]

This understanding shows the depth of the enslaved's bondage. The practice of chattel slavery in America ensnares the body, mind, and spirit, that which comprises the soul. Since human beings are, according to Nee, soulical by nature, therefore it is the human soul that is impacted within the world as it simultaneously impacts the world. People "often account what is soulical as spiritual," which dislocates the severity and affront of the slavocracy.[7] The breath breathed in the beginning is a transracial breath. Everyone is in possession of it. This breath is what unifies all humanity. The challenge with American imperial capitalistic culture is that the very nature of the system requires some group to dominate or conquer another. Within the context of American history, the moral stance taken to justify actions of unjust conquest is divine right, whether the stance is labeled "for queen and country" or "westward expansion." In other words, it is a God-given right for one people/group to inherit the land thereby causing a lesser people/group to remain disinherited. The call for a rebirth, then, is a call to deconstruct the normative conceptualization of divine right to embrace the radical reformation espoused by these courageous writers of the nineteenth century. This radical reformation requires a shift in how black people in America view themselves and white Americans. Simultaneously, it involves an evolution in how white Americans view and understand the other. Sometimes the response is not obvious and comes from an unlikely source during the American Slavocracy. Phillis Wheatley literally constructs perspectives of liberation with theological foundations countering the soteriological Eurocentric notions of divine election prevalent during the period and aimed at liberating an oppressed people socially, economically, and politically.

One day while I was conversing with scholar and Dean of the Morehouse School of Religion Joseph Norman Evans, he suggested that Alexander Crummell and W. E. B. Du Bois in particular are responsible for the genesis and foundation of black liberation theology. This assertion led me to investigate conversations, theories, and works that might have emerged prior to the foundational conversations that inform James Cone's work. Most scholarly works that seek to engage liberation theology tend to invoke the name and cultural critiques of James Cone as their foundation. After my conversation with Evans, I was interested in focusing less on Cone as the father of liberation theology and more on his process for developing a liberation theology. Further, I wanted to see how African American writers, namely Phillis Wheatley (among others), whose works predate Cone's formalization of his theology of liberation, use certain methods of cultural critique to present a liberation perspective that indirectly could have informed Cone's work.[8]

Cone creates his new platform during the Black Power Movement by reorienting the process of developing a theology. Traditionally, theological arguments were articulated by starting with a theory and applying it to the biblical narrative, thereby arriving at a point of implementation or interrogation that fits a particular people/group or that has some sort of universal application. According to Matthew Rose, theologian Karl Barth sought to liberate "Christian theology from restrictive modern habits of mind,"[9] propositions purported by enlightenment philosophers such as Hegel, Kant, Descartes, and Hume. Barth's theology, however, is rooted in God's self-expression in history alone, which proves problematic when engaging the black experience in America because Barth presents a liberation theology that is "trapped within the immanent confines of secular reason."[10] By stripping the individual's necessity to reason through an articulation of the being of God, Barth actually reifies some of what he is seeking to discredit. For Barth, revelation dismisses the human subject and is limited to what God decides to reveal within the confines of the Europeanized historical Jesus Christ. Cone realizes that this process does not suffice for black people in America. Reading, analyzing, and critiquing the saga of black people's experience in America and relating to it, he weds the black experience to the biblical experience to arrive at an acceptable and transformational theoretical home for the American Negro and comes to love the being of God, which he can articulate.

While Wheatley's process probably was not as methodic and predictable, it is nonetheless relevant. Wheatley articulates a form of liberation theology (what I am calling a liberation perspective) that sets the stage that allows Cone to formalize liberation theology, not unlike Du Bois and his peers' critiques of dominant Western constructions of God and humanity. Whereas Cone's liberation theology is deliberately scholarly, Wheatley presents nuanced and creative perspectives of liberation in her literary works, which can be extracted through a cultural/theological (or maybe both) critique, which she accomplishes through her neoclassical approach that is informed by her knowledge and awareness of Latin.

Her engagement with her historical culture is evidenced in her analysis of the Revolutionary period (1770–1783), which sets the stage for American Reconstruction over a century later. The Revolutionary period is significant because Phillis Wheatley wrote and published *Poems on Various Subjects Religious and Moral* in the years leading up to the war. With the war breaking out in 1775, it can be argued that much of Wheatley's poetry speaks to the rising tensions in America at this time, particularly as America seeks to distinctly define the nation as different and separate from England. One of the key points of contention was the desire for separation from the Church of England and the oppressive nature of the legalistic polity therein. From this time forward, Americans have sought to define and redefine who God is and how humankind interacts or is in relationship with this God and each other. With the eventual loss (in theory) of the slavocracy, white people need to reconceptualize or redefine the black body, thereby redefining black humanity.

You Must Be Born Again could be viewed by some, particularly those in literary studies, as a critical engagement with the black aesthetic or aesthetics in general. I am certainly informed by the transitional works of Larry Neal, Addison Gayle, Amiri Baraka, and April C. E. Langley. I fully understand there is a continued need to make visible both the scholarship on eighteenth-century African American literature and the aesthetic worth of black art from that period. This work seeks to engage the ongoing aesthetic argument by examining what I am calling four theoretical threads I see converging to define or uncover a prophetic plea for an American rebirth through Wheatley's poetics.

The first thread is that of aesthetics in eighteenth-century America. Scholars like Edward Cahill, Edward Larkin, Christopher Castiglia, and April

C. E. Langley offer nuanced and historically committed assessments of the eighteenth-century aesthetic moment. Both Cahill and Larkin give us a solid working definition of aesthetics in eighteenth-century American literature, noting that it is "concerned with the range of meanings" as it pertains to both "feeling" and "form."[11] They further suggest that aesthetics studies provides a lens for merging history and the social through literary criticism. In this way, aesthetics studies is able to do significant cultural work. Despite this positive potential for aesthetics, they do not overlook the traditional trinity of pitfalls: elitism and triviality, conceptual ambiguity, and material conditions. When aesthetics begins doing cultural work, there emerges a new formalism, which is challenged by some scholars. Jane Tomkins, in *Sensational Designs*, notes, "novels and stories should be studied not because they manage to escape the limitations of their particular time and place, but because they offer powerful examples of the way a culture thinks about itself, articulating and proposing solutions for the problems that shape a particular historical moment."[12] Though her assessment can be read as an indictment on aesthetics, her critique actually serves as a gateway for a reengaged aesthetic critique that chooses to see those who are often overlooked and/or cast aside as other. In this way, truth clears a path toward liberation and inclusion, thereby countering elitism and triviality. Additionally, if the specific culture or community is the arena of critical engagement, there is much less ambiguity and a commitment of certain institutions, according to Cahill and Larkin, to support these academic efforts.[13]

Given some of the challenges and gaps in aesthetic criticism, Castiglia seeks to refocus the conversation squarely on the imagination, both in creation and interpretation. I believe this is a significant notion when relating to poetry, for poetic verse by and large is dependent (as is most art) on the imagination. It only makes sense, then, that the evaluator of art should have an appreciation for the imagination. He notes that literary criticism is headed in an imaginative direction, a course that is winding toward what Ernst Bloch has termed the "not-yet-real."[14] Castiglia's read of the cultural criticism climate of the eighteenth century culminates in what is the "coexistence of poetic and revolutionary imagination" that ultimately borders on the prophetic.[15]

With the guardrails taken off of the art as critically engaged, the window is open for an articulation of and appreciation for the black aesthetic. April C. E. Langley unlocks discourse of the other through her interpretation of the black aesthetic. She traces it "through its triangular engagement with the languages, cultures, and experiences of Africa, Europe, and North America."[16] She systematically explores the African presence in early American literature and culture, locates "elements of a developing eighteenth-century black aesthetic," and relocates "Africa within African American literature."[17] Her engagement with black aesthetics is directly and importantly connected to identity politics.

The second thread is the politics of identity. Personhood or ontological self-worth is something that is necessary to critically engage early American literature and culture. James Olney, Margaret Miles, Kelly Brown Douglas, and Wendy Raphael Roberts each engage identity politics in ways that help to inform how *You Must Be Born Again* interrogates Phillis Wheatley's presentation of herself through her poetry. Though the phrase "I was born" is most commonly associated as a convention of the emancipatory or slave narrative genre, it has import for my engagement with Wheatley's poetics. James Olney explores these conventions and suggests why the opening "I was born" statement is both significant and troubling. He notes,

> We can see the necessity for this first and most basic assertion on the part of the ex-slave in the contrary situation of an autobiographer like Benjamin Franklin. While any reader was free to doubt the motives of Franklin's memoir, no one could doubt his existence, and so Franklin begins not with any claims or proofs that he was born and now really exists but with an explanation of why he has chosen to write such a document as the one in hand. With the ex-slave, however, it was his existence and his identity, not his reasons for writing, that were called into question.[18]

If it was necessary in the nineteenth century, it was also necessary in the eighteenth century. *You Must Be Born Again* suggests that blacks in America have had to and continue to have to justify their existence and worth.

The necessary negotiation of the black body is significant for engaging the eighteenth-century slavocracy in America. Body theology is a philosophical thread that weaves throughout American culture and history and is typically articulated by the dominant culture. According to Margaret Miles, "All Christian theology is body theology in that its distinctive characteristic is affirmation of the permanent integrity of the human body as given in creation, affirmed in the incarnation of Jesus Christ, nourished in the sacraments of the Christian churches, and to be glorified in the resurrection of the body."[19] If the primary contention of body theology is the "permanent integrity of the human body," the defining of the human body as anything but significant and valuable in relation to another human body is disingenuous to God as creator of all humanity. Global citizens began determining bodily value in recent history during the Atlantic Slave Trade when bodies were bought and sold for free labor. The adherence to body theology does not cease in this scenario; it is simply redefined. A more contemporary understanding of body theology is that it refers to "theological statements that specifically address questions related to personal and social attitudes towards the body, moral decisions regarding one's own body and those of other human beings, and theological concern about the physical conditions in which human beings live and work."[20] Europeans participating in the Slave Trade and subsequent slave masters throughout the Americas made "moral decisions" about the black body and then developed a theology of the black body that was different from that of the white body. The white body is valuable, and the black body is serviceable or useful for labor; hence, the white body is preferred or favored especially by God. This negotiation of the black body is the source of Westernized notions of divine right. The moral decisions result in a corrupt lived ethic, which is what Wheatley is actively writing against.

Significantly, theology of the black body is best defined to date by Kelly Brown Douglas, who suggests that there is historical evidence supporting an understanding of black life in America as a bodily saga. Black people have been defined by the position of their bodies, socially, economically, and spiritually. The black body arrives on American soil as chattel, and the positioning of the black body as such results in a construction on inherent guilt.[21] The black body's "classification as chattel is also that which substantiates the fundamental distinction between the white body and the black body."[22] As chattel, black people have had no right to possess land and other material things nor themselves. As chattel, black people were forced to exist without acknowledgment of their personhood or ability to access resources available to American citizens. Black people, as chattel, belong to someone. In the American historical landscape, black people belong to white people. This is significant because whiteness is reliant on blackness for its substantiation and legitimization.

In *Awakening Verse*, Wendy Raphael Roberts suggests Wheatley engages in revival poetics on her terms. Her argument supports the notion that Wheatley's "I was born" statement emerges imaginatively through an act of self-creation and self-definition. She states that Wheatley invents an adaptable persona—the Ethiop—who is able to engage the culture and critique its flaws in ways her white counterparts could not. Roberts points toward a new revivalism that could only be proffered by this invented Ethiop. Significantly, Wheatley's nonconformist approach to poetry in general and Roberts's analysis of her approach to "On the Death of the Reverend Mr. George Whitefield" in particular expresses the Ethiop's voice and worth. It is another iteration of her "I was born" statement. This is a point I will return to in chapter 2, "Encountering God through the Preacher," where I give an analysis of the influence Whitefield had on Wheatley.

Wheatley consistently pushes against the barriers of convention to define herself amid harsh critiques of influential figures such as Thomas Jefferson who "insists that [she] is the category of people with religious capacity but not intellectual and refined aesthetic capacity."[23] It is as though Jefferson is making Wheatley out to be the representative of all people who look like her. Echoes of Anna Julia Cooper ring through an historical future moment enabling Wheatley to utter, "When and where I enter, the race enters with me."[24] But, what is Wheatley entering with? Who or what tradition(s) is she bringing with her?

The third thread is a reclamation of African ways of cultural engagement. Here, I return to Langley and *The Black Aesthetic Unbound*, particularly because of the sagacious and nuanced manner in which she articulates Wheatley's quest to break out of the conventional identity markers prescribed for her as poet-minister within some predetermined white evangelical compassionate conservative framework. Langley notes Wheatley's approach or "ways . . . move beyond interpretations that suggest a one-on-one correspondence or merely parallel view of similar models of power relationships."[25] The "way" Wheatley chooses is that of Senegambian poetics, which "enable her to participate simultaneously in both and Africanist and Americanist discourse—without negating either."[26] This expression of Wheatley's poetics opens the door for a transgressive prophetic instantiation that is communal and trans-American. It is Africentric.

To further engage Wheatley's Africentrism, I turn to Ayi Kwei Armah and *The Eloquence of the Scribes* to help unlock the Ethiop or Griotte within Wheatley's poetics. Armah helps pave the critical path of liberation within an Africanist framework. Wheatley as Griotte or Jaliyaa is critical of the American culture and consistent in her dual commitment at African in America, much like the ancient Hebrew prophets, all the while embodying true "Christian" virtue and simultaneously complicating it. As I articulate in chapter 4, the goddess Maât serves as representative of virtue for Wheatley. She merges her Africanist self with her Americanist self to create a new morality that proves to be Africentric.

Wheatley's Africanist presence is undeniable in her poetry, a point that is also effectively lifted by Katherine Clay Bassard in *Spiritual Interrogations*. She buttresses her engagement with Wheatley through her interpretation of the language of arrival, seeking to ask the epistemological question of whether or not Wheatley knew what she was doing. As asked earlier, What is Wheatley entering with? For Bassard, coupled with this are, as with all instances of arrival, the politics of arrival. The insertion of the other to a normed space. Bassard weaves Morrison's "Africanist presence" with Du Bois's "double-consciousness" noting:

> If "whiteness" comes into being as a reaction to the presence of "blackness," then African Americanism must be more than simply a reaction to that reaction. In fact, it is a vantage point—Du Bois called it "double consciousness"—that sees the construction of Whiteness, catches it, if you will, in its reflexive

posture vis-à-vis its construction of a discourse of blackness as a discourse of difference.[27]

Blackness being foundational as opposed to reactionary is significant. Blackness, the "Africanist presence," is thereby intrinsically creative. Black presence forces white people to create whiteness. The othered black presence then must create a space for itself, as space of being. Wheatley is a creator of this type of being-space through her prophetic poetics that simultaneously dismantles institutional whiteness and carves out avenues for authentic black expressive passage. As Bassard suggests, Wheatley "is both writer and theorizer of African Americanism, a discourse she helped to create."[28] I would add, she is also the creator of liberation theology as we have come to know it in an American context, as articulated through art.

The fourth and final thread is the poet's voice. More specifically it is the prophetic voice. The prophetic has been negotiated throughout history, dating back to ancient civilizations. *You Must Be Born Again* in no way intends to rehearse every debate, but it does seek to enter the conversation through the long-standing discipline of hermeneutics, particularly as it relates to the interpretation of texts based on the baggage or worldview the reader brings to the text. I analyze this idea of speech, particularly prophetic speech, extensively in chapter 1 in conversation with Dolan Hubbard, Richard Lischer, Walter Brueggemann, and Charles Long. Importantly, my engagement with the prophetic is through both theological and literary discourse. There is a necessity to keep the two in connection to gain a truer understanding of how the prophetic operates through speech, written or oral.

The First Amendment has emerged or at least been amplified as a hot-button topic in the "age of social media." Attention is drawn on nearly every major news outlet to people's voices. The freedom of speech, religion, and the press is at the core of what it means to be a land of liberty. The amendment, however, omits a principal qualifier—namely, to whom these freedoms apply: "Congress shall make no law respecting an establishment of religion or prohibiting the free exercise thereof; or abridging the freedom of speech, or of the press; or the right of the people peaceably to assemble, and to petition the Government for a redress of grievances."[29] Granted, to find the qualifier, one simply need look at the opening lines of the Constitution: "We the People of the United States, in Order to form a more perfect Union, establish Justice, insure domestic Tranquility, provide for the common defence, promote the general Welfare, and secure the Blessings of Liberty to ourselves and our Posterity, do ordain and establish this Constitution for the United States of America."[30] The pledge to "secure the Blessings of Liberty to ourselves and our Posterity" is significant, for it indicates for whom liberty is available. Importantly, Phillis Wheatley publishes *Poems on Various Subjects* in 1773, some fourteen years before the framing of the Constitution[31] and three years before the document known as the United States Declaration of Independence was presented to the Continental Congress. There was an opportunity for the framers and, in particular, the Committee of Five to write all people into the founding documents of a new and progressive nation. Perhaps Thomas Jefferson's worldview proved most influential, for there are

> [d]eep rooted prejudices entertained by the whites . . . the real distinctions which nature has made. . . . The first difference which strikes us is that of colour. Whether the black of the negro resides in the reticular membrane between the skin and scarf-skin, or in the scarf-skin itself; whether it proceeds from the colour of the blood, the colour of the bile, or from that of some other secretion, the difference is fixed in nature, and is as real as if its seat and cause were better known to us.[32]

Jefferson continues with a series of leading questions that serve as qualifiers for the black body's exclusion from the universal freedoms established within America:

> And is this difference of no importance? Is it not the foundation of a greater or less share of beauty in the two races? Are not the fine mixtures of red and white, the expressions of every passion by greater or less suffusions of colour in the one, preferable to that eternal monotony, which reigns in the countenances, that immovable veil of black which covers all the emotions of the other race? . . . The circumstance of superior beauty, is thought worthy attention in the propagation of our horses, dogs, and other domestic animals; why not in that of man?[33]

This reasoning expressed by one of the "founding fathers" of this nation, a slaveholder himself, proves to expose the lengths to which white men were willing to go to exclude the "domestic animals" known as Blacks in America from the cultural narrative. For these reasons and many others, the founding documents of this nation are proven to be prejudiced at best and hypocritical at worst.

Despite the opening lines of the Declaration of Independence and the Preamble of the Constitution, Black writers have sought to present a prescriptive alternative standard for equality, justice, and national identity. Wheatley sagaciously exposes "what moves at the margin" to provide insights for a developing nation.[34] She presents a proposal for inclusion, living into the politics of respectability though she is not invited to sit at the table. Such is the reality of the influence of the prophet. As one called to speak truth to power, the reception is often cold or noncommittal. Wheatley seeks to cast a new reality for America.

The theology developed by Europeans, particularly white people in America, began with these notions of superiority and divine right. Contrastingly, for black people, as according to Cone's methodology, theologies are constructed out of the experiences of the group of people. From the black perspective, there emerges undoubtedly a theology of the black body resulting from chattel slavery and oppression experienced in America. This theology of the black body differs significantly from that developed by white people based on their moral decisions. It is through the rhetoric and perspectives of liberation that this articulation is most vehemently expressed. For example, liberation theologies are constructed to "advocate the alleviation of oppressive political structures and reject the spiritualization of the Christian message."[35] As a type of body theology, then, liberation theology takes as its framework "a Christian evaluation of the value and significance of the human body as the good creation of God, worthy of respectful care."[36] For these reasons, black liberation theology focuses on the resistance to, removal of, and retaliation against any constrictive and restrictive ideologies (morality), policies, and practices (ethics) that threaten or devalue the "permanent integrity of the human body."[37] The black body within the framework of black liberation theology is of equal value to all other bodies, a point emphasized throughout my interrogation of the various works by Wheatley.

American Eurocentric soteriology suggests God has shown special favor or grace upon those of European descent, reaffirming the white American body theology. This special favor or divine right is a direct result of the power struggle between white people and black people in America. Of course, this power struggle is one-sided. White people felt the need to firmly establish who they are and what place they hold in society and, in so doing, created a power struggle between white people and non-white people in America, a struggle that continues today. Whereas white people relied on their consistent oppression of black people to establish and maintain their sense of power, black people practiced self-empowerment. This practice proved problematic for the white people who were in power because it emerges outside of the white realm of acceptability and in essence separates the body from the soul.[38] Black people asserting themselves as powerful despite white oppression and the white Christian message encroached on the boundaries set up by white Christian theology. As C. Eric Lincoln notes, the Puritans were "a closed-membership organization" fully operating within the bounds of what they declared their divine right.[39] This understanding of the church and of New Testament Christianity (as privileging a chosen elect) could be the genesis of the breakdown of the church as an American institution. A belief in exceptionalism that justifies American conquest is disingenuous to the original intent of the first-century church.[40] Therefore, today many churches (black and white) suffer from being exclusionary and, thereby, distanced from the original mission. The closed-membership model firmly imbeds separation of cultures, races, religions, and social backgrounds. It is a type of cheap grace, a self-proclaimed exclusivity, an extremist version of the Calvinist doctrine of election; it is what Dietrich Bonhoeffer has deemed grace or favor without discipleship.[41] In other words, Eurocentric soteriology, in its bastardized form, that is found throughout the annals of American history and literature, preaches a righteousness without responsibility, a crown without a cross, elitism with little critical engagement, and privilege without the practice of true community. It is as if white America, particularly the American South, during the latter half of the nineteenth century practiced worth righteousness as opposed to works righteousness.[42] Their entitlement brought instant worth, which bred a sense of complacency and misguided or unbridled recklessness presented in soteriological form. White people were/are favored because God and the Bible have deemed it so. Therefore, white people in America act accordingly, by placing black people and redefining personhood, and thereby the black body, to serve their culturally exclusive soteriological ends.

Writers like Phillis Wheatley (I would even add David Walker, Maria Stewart, Frederick Douglass, and Charles Chesnutt) attempt to counter notions of divine election based solely on race by creatively articulating alternative possibilities for personhood, community, and ultimately justification. Wheatley and her co-laborers' proposed processes differ, but their conceptual framework is the same. For too long, the American literary landscape has attempted to reify theoretical perceptions of whiteness in America to maintain a "pure" canon. Much of the literature taught and critically examined is Eurocentric, and those works that are not Eurocentric are often engaged and critiqued using a Eurocentric lens. Hence, *You Must Be Born Again* seeks to present a writer who is, at times, recognized within the American literary canon and at other times (depending on the radical nature of the work) relegated to the margins of the canon. Specifically, I analyze/include both traditionally canonized works and less familiar works by Wheatley. Through her works, she calls for an ethical rebirth to restore the original intent for humanity—equality.

You Must Be Born Again intends to take the reader on a journey through the mind and pen of Phillis Wheatley while defining some key terms and concepts, thereby reintroducing the reader to the poet. In fact, I consider Wheatley to be a Poet-Theologian, positioning her as one uniquely anointed or qualified (not by any traditional academic or professional standards) to speak to the social issues of her day and beyond. As Poet-Theologian, she stands at the intersection of the reality experienced within a developing, ingenuine America and the hope of an American potentiality. In chapter 2, I discuss the influence of the Gospel preacher and the Gospel preaching tradition on Wheatley's worldview and outlook as it pertains to human dignity and responsibility. The

Preacher-Poet, in this instance, serves as the conduit for the positive change within society. Building upon the influences in Wheatley's life, chapter 3 discusses the power of her pen, which is her spoken word. Traditionally, the spoken word carries with it a heightened sense of urgency often not communicated as forcefully or impactfully on the page. Wheatley, however, is able to write in such a way that the emotions, inflections, and convections seem to leap from the pages. The spoken word is inherently creative, and Wheatley consistently uses her words to create and re-create.

In chapters 4 and 5, I deal with two key concepts that are woven throughout the entirety of this project but are dealt with in detail within these chapters—creation and salvation. In these two chapters, I analyze Wheatley's engagement with humanity through the doctrines of creation and salvation, noting how she directly and decidedly combats notions of divine right in "On the Works of Providence," inclusive of giving a methodology for reclaiming the best of humanity as negotiated through the salvific work of Christ.

I close my engagement with Wheatley by exploring the story behind the voice and uncovering Wheatley's universalist plea to position the black body as a meaningful contributor to American culture and society. As Poet-Preacher and Poet-Theologian, Phillis Wheatley seeks to unite a bifurcated nation, understanding, in the final instance, that "unto whomsoever much is given, of him shall be much required."[43]

My hope is that *You Must Be Born Again* is far-reaching. I believe it will be helpful for seminary, literary, and African American Studies students. In addition, pastors and social activists will hopefully glean tools for leadership and framing social agendas. Further, anyone interested in literature as a social/theological tool as well as those interested in the intersections among race, racism, ethics, theology, and whiteness will be able to be inspired by the words and underlying intentions of Phillis Wheatley's seminal work through a fresh lens.

NOTES

1. Very recently, many scholars prefer referring to Wheatley as Wheatley Peters, noting her marriage to John Peters in 1778. I use Wheatley throughout primarily because each work I engage was composed by "Phillis Wheatley" prior to her marriage.

2. I could note here the name of the church. Significantly, a church named "New South" in the North is significant. Perhaps, the rationale lies in the desire, need, and mandate to create a "New South" that is representative of the biblical understanding of community among all peoples. Yet, Wheatley is still enslaved. This is the unfortunate reality of some abolitionist circles in the North.

3. Scheick, "Subjection and Prophecy," 123.
4. Gen. 1:26–2:7 (KJV).
5. "May the God of peace himself sanctify you wholly; and may your spirit and soul and body be kept sound and blameless at the coming of our Lord Jesus Christ" (1 Thess. 5:23 KJV).
6. Nee, *Spiritual Man*, 25.
7. Nee, 25.
8. Though the focus of this project is Wheatley, there is an historical continuum of theological thought within literary works by Black writers that promotes liberation that includes the works of Douglass, Walker, Stewart, Chesnutt, Du Bois, Harper, Cooper, and others.
9. Rose, "Karl Barth's Failure," 39.
10. Rose, 43.
11. Cahill and Larkin, "Aesthetics, Feeling, and Form," 243.
12. Tomkins, *Sensational Designs*, xi.
13. See Cahill and Larkin, "Aesthetics, Feeling, and Form."
14. Castiglia, "Revolution Is a Fiction," 403.
15. Castiglia, 406.
16. Langley, *The Black Aesthetic Unbound*, 2.
17. Langley, 2–3.
18. Olney, "'I Was Born,'" 53.
19. Miles, "Body Theology," 77.
20. Miles, 77.
21. Douglas, *Stand Your Ground*, 53.
22. Douglas, 53.
23. Roberts, *Awakening Verse*, 129.
24. Cooper, *The Voice of Anna Julia Cooper*, 63.
25. Langley, 72.
26. Langley, 73.
27. Bassard, *Spiritual Interrogations*, 70.
28. Bassard, 32.
29. U.S. Constitution, amendment I.
30. U.S. Constitution, Preamble.
31. Sixteen years prior to its going into effect, March 4, 1789.
32. Jefferson, *Notes on the State of Virginia*, 138.
33. Jefferson, 138.
34. In her Nobel lecture, Toni Morrison states, "Tell us what the world has been to you in the dark places and in the light. Don't tell us what to believe, what to fear. Show us belief's wide skirt and the stitch that unravels fear's caul. . . . Tell us what it is to be a woman so that we may know what it is to be a man. What moves at the margin. What it is to have no home in this place. To be set adrift from the one you knew. What it is to live at the edge of towns that cannot bear your company" (206). *What Moves at the Margin: Selected Nonfiction.* (Jackson: University of Mississippi Press, 2008).
35. Miles, 77.

36. Miles, 77.
37. Miles, 77.
38. Bassard, 60.
39. Lincoln, "The Development of Black Religion in America," 12.
40. In the Old Testament, God declared Israel as God's chosen people. Throughout the Old Testament, we see Israel given land that is already inhabited. Often these lands are taken by force and involves bloodshed. However, by the time of the emergence of the church in the New Testament, we see grace enacted by God. Though God does not direct God's people in the New Testament to "take the land," God does declare those who follow Christ as "a chosen generation" (1 Pet. 2:9a). This notion of "chosen-ness" informs the church's collective theology.
41. Dietrich Bonhoeffer notes, "Cheap grace means grace sold on the market like cheapjacks' wares. . . . Cheap grace is the preaching of forgiveness without requiring repentance, baptism without church discipline, Communion without confession, absolution without personal confession. Cheap grace is grace without discipleship, grace without the cross, grace without Jesus Christ, living and incarnate" (*The Cost of Discipleship*, trans. Reginald H. Fuller [New York: Macmillan, 1959], 35–36).
42. Worth righteousness undergirds white people's racialized morality, but it is works righteousness that requires an ethical basis for communal existence.
43. Lk. 12:48 (KJV).

Chapter 1

Phillis Wheatley, the Poet-Theologian

For some, being a theologian is not inherently academic. In fact, it can be argued that all human beings are capable of being a theologian. Howard Stone and James Duke proffer, "To be a Christian at all is to be a theologian. There are no exceptions."[1] I further contend that to be aware of one's humanity is to be a theologian. Importantly, one's religious location/home does not innately matter, for the orientation of one's reflection is most significant. We are all, in some way, ultimately concerned beyond ourselves.[2] Theological reflection, then, is the process of "working with various materials or resources, applying certain skills that can be learned and honed overtime by concentration and practice."[3] If theological reflection is learned through concentration and practice, it begins with the imagination. Walter Brueggemann, reflecting on his 1978 publication *The Prophetic Imagination,* notes that the pairing of those words "prophetic" and "imagination" was somewhat coincidental yet meaningful:

> To qualify "prophetic" by "imagination" is to dig deeper than moral earnestness into the notion of playful, venturesome probing into the unknown that requires poetic utterance and that evokes daring images and metaphors, all in the service of an elusiveness out beyond royal totalism. To evade royal totalism requires an emancipated imagination that refuses the domesticated categories of settled control.[4]

He continues, "On the other hand, to qualify the term 'imagination' by the adjective 'prophetic' delivers imagination from sheer fantasy into a world of covenantal engagement that features YHWH as the compelling partner of both the human prophetic utterer and those who heard the prophetic utterance in serious ways."[5] The imagination, then, serves as the seat of transformative engagement with God and humanity. As Brueggemann notes, there is a "venturesome probing" through "poetic utterance" required to articulate the new, as yet unknown reality. This reality can only be interpreted with an "emancipated imagination" that is not subject to the power structures that exist. The transgressive and playful "poetic utterance" is the result of a willing vessel composing with the divine for humanity. For these reasons, the poet is uniquely positioned and primed to be a theologian.

In the prefatory authentication of Phillis Wheatley's *Poems on Various Subjects, Religious and Moral*, John Wheatley, her master, writes, "As to her writing, her own curiosity led her to it."[6] The "it" John Wheatley references is writing as a discipline. He positions her as a self-taught poet who sought to perfect her craft through exploration. He mentions her "great Inclination to learn Latin in addition to the English language."[7] The question that arises from his statement of authentication, however, is what lies beyond the "it" of Phillis Wheatley's curiosity? Richard Lischer, in his book *The End of Words: The Language of Reconciliation in a Culture of Violence*, suggests that there is a transaction that takes place at the end of words that has the potential to be suggestive, engaging, and even transformative. He intimates, "The poet says 'the end is where we start from' and that is true for preachers as well."[8] The idea is that in times of trauma and tragedy there is a wall of sorts erected to prevent words' effectiveness. The words have a tendency, in these moments, to sound hollow and empty; "[t]he proclamation of God's justice or God's love meets a wall of resistance first in the throat of the proclaimer, then in the ears of the hearer."[9] Lischer goes on to state:

> When true convictions give way to bigger and bigger lies told with increasingly passionate intensity, the poet knows that it is time to keep silence. Later in the century, certain theologians and preachers would join the poets in denouncing the corruption of language. When the message of Jesus Christ can be Nazified or made the tool of racism, anti-Semitism, apartheid, or capitalism, it is time for preachers to shut up and take stock of themselves. Before any prophet speaks, the prophet is absolutely positive that he or she must *not* speak.[10]

It is in the moments of internal solitary confinement that the poet and the preacher become aware of the people's arrival at "the end of words" and the preacher-poet's inadequacy to speak in such times.[11] Yet, in these moments of internal solitary confinement erupts a certain "curiosity," which is really an internal compulsion from the Muses, the Spirit, the gods that imbue the poet and the preacher with a unique vision that breaks the bounds of words.

The "it" of Wheatley's "curiosity" is the need to imagine a new world. Her need to imagine an alternate reality is not uncommon for the slave, yet the vehicle through which she chooses to inscribe and thereby articulate that new reality is unique and trailblazing. As, arguably, the first black woman to publish a collection of poetry, Wheatley sets a transgressive liberative stage for those who would follow. Houston Baker, appropriating Sterling Stuckey's analysis, notes, "The slave, staring into the heart of whiteness around [her], must have felt as though [she] had been flung into existence without a human purpose."[12] Baker suggests that Wheatley, confronted with such a reality, chooses to gaze idealistically back to Africa without confronting her current reality and certainly not offering an alternative reality within America.

Clearly, one sees that Wheatley does not readily adopt "the god of the enslaver as solace."[13] She does not simply gaze forward to a hopeful apocalyptic rapture that would grant her freedom either. So, if Wheatley does not retreat to Africa, as Baker and Stuckey suggest; and, if she does not choose to complacently adopt the reality of her present; and, if she does not place her hope in an ethereal anticipation of a God-directed/instituted apocalypse, where does she turn? Wheatley, unlike Douglass who would follow her, chooses to write her personhood into the fabric of late-eighteenth-century American culture. Baker rightly articulates, "and unlike white Americans who could assume literacy and familiarity with existing literary models as norms, the slave found himself without a system of written language.... He first had to seize the word. His being had to erupt from nothingness. Only by grasping the word could he engage in the speech acts that would ultimately define his selfhood."[14] The mere act of Wheatley choosing to "grasp the word" for the sake of articulating a new reality that begins with redefining her personhood and culminates with her plea for a radical reconstruction of communal relations in America is proof of her commitment to "it." The "it" Wheatley is seeking to articulate is the "not-yet-real" Ernst Bloch has named. As Wheatley occupies the space of preacher-poet, she grapples with her "existing reality in order to create a pure ideal reality."[15] What emerges is "the coexistence of poetic and revolutionary imagination,"[16] what Brueggemann would term the prophetic imagination.

For Wheatley, the "it" is more than the word on the page, but "it" is about the transaction or exchange that results when the word is articulated in artistic form. In this sense, "it" is more akin to the Word made flesh. Her poetry, as the tangible expression of her curiosity or imagination, is her positing of her theological reflection, as presented through her poetry, becomes the artistic articulation of who God is and how that God interacts with humanity. Further, she is making bold recommendations throughout. It is her literary imagination that drives her pen, hence the reason many readers and scholars have overlooked or misrepresented her poetic theology.

In *The Sermon and the African American Literary Imagination*, Dolan Hubbard suggests that the fictional literature of several African Americans sets the navigator compass for emerging out of the oppressive underbelly of American culture in order to forge a new reality inside of America. Black people, in essence, are stuck in a created world not of their own, "lost souls trapped in the American Dream."[17] Black writers, like black preachers, are tasked with breaking the bonds of entrapment while presenting a nuanced alternative "Dream" that uplifts the black culture while constructively critiquing the dominant culture. The preacher sagaciously articulates a new world by

> [s]tepping out of darkness—itself a symbol of the experience of Africans in America—the preacher imposes a unity of meaning upon what Hayden White refers to as "the chaos of history." The preacher, as archetypal performer, critiques the metaphorical system in which both the blackness of the corporate community and its experiences have been valorized by the dominant culture as a "natural" absence from the historical realm. As a result of this "natural" absence, the black sermon in its totality must be seen as an interjection rather than as a declaration.[18]

In this sense, the preacher serves as the drum major for the culture, giving cues to the listening ear as to the moral standing required to live and live free within society. There is authority and influence within the sermonic discourse that is "so deeply embedded in the black psyche that, whether one be preacher, pimp, or poet, one's status in the black community is often measured by how fluent one is in the collective, communal oral literature. The black sermon is the heroic voice of black America."[19] It is through the preacher's oratory that the people gain the insight and courage to "break free from economic, psychological, and spatial immobility."[20] The sermon within the black tradition is structured, typically, to bring hope and a challenge. This dynamic has occurred throughout the history of blacks in America; however, does it change or diverge when the proclamation shifts from oral to written?

Dr. Martin Luther King Jr. states in the preface of *Strength to Love* he had "been rather reluctant to have a volume of sermons printed. My misgivings have grown out of the fact that a sermon is not an essay to be read but a discourse to be heard. It should be a convincing appeal to a listening congregation. Therefore, a sermon is directed toward the listening ear rather than the reading eye."[21] His convictions call into question the effectiveness of the written sermon. As a preacher myself, I often wrestle with this startling reality/conundrum. I understand the call and response tradition of the black church, the jazziness of the preaching moment, the blue notes articulated and witnessed, and the celebratory hope that is offered. Yet, as a theologian and scholar, I also understand the need for the written sermon and not just for posterity's sake. There is something else preserved in the written word. The only way to really describe it is to bind the effect of the written sermon with that of the *Holy Bible*. Biblical stories/passages contain more than polished prose and poignant poetry. Beyond the script is a type of ether, a spiritual quality that evokes a reaction that pushes beyond mere reader-response.

There is a collecting and a compelling that reaches through the printed words on the page to engage each reader in a tailored manner. Your reaction will not necessarily be my reaction and vice versa. Nevertheless, all who read it will arrive at some distinct destination.

I use this analogy because the books of the Bible were originally written to be read aloud, as stories—literary text—and the Bible has fairly recently (within the last four hundred years) become widely accessible to a large reading audience. The educated, by and large, have been the ones with consistent access to the written text of the Bible. The masses, however, heard the word before they ever read the word. For these reasons, King's hesitance is significant, for you cannot duplicate the atmosphere of a church, synagogue, temple, or other venue where people are gathered around a voice. However, I believe there is another type of engagement that can be had through the written word that proves to be similarly effectual for the preacher/writer and the hearer/reader. Again, Lischer's words inspire that, even in the written form, there is a type of critical engagement that "dance[s] just beyond the limits of words."[22] Even with a distant audience, I argue the poet-theologian/poet-preacher and readers are "engaged in a dynamic exchange" that is transformative, communal, and creational.[23] It is the written word that breaks beyond the boundaries of place and time that presents what Hortense Spillers (speaking of the oral sermon as a type of poetry) suggests is "not simply an exegetical, theological presentation, but a complete expression of a gamut of emotions whose central form is the narrative and whose end is cathartic release. In that regard the sermon is an instrument of a collective catharsis, binding once again the isolated members of community."[24] In this way, the poet is a type of complement to the preacher. In fact, Ralph Waldo Emerson suggests that the poet is one of the only members of society that sees and interprets the world rightly.

> The poet is the sayer, the namer, and represents beauty. He is a sovereign and stands on the centre.... Therefore the poet is not any permissive potentate, but is emporer in his own right. Criticism is infested with the cant of materialism, which assumes that manual skill and activity is the first merit of all men, and disparages such as say and do not, overlooking the fact, that some men, namely, poets, are natural sayers, sent into the world to the end of expression, and confounds them with those whose province is action.... The sign and credentials of the poet are, that he announces that which no man foretold. He is the true and only doctor; he knows and tells; he is the only teller of news, for he was present and privy to the appearance which he describes. He is a beholder of ideas, and an utterer of the necessary and casual. For we do not speak now of men of poetical talents, or of industry and skill in metre, but of the true poet.[25]

The poet, then, is not merely a rhetorical wordsmith; rather the poet is the one that understands his or her giftedness is reliant on inspiration. This is a point I will return to later in this chapter. The preacher as poet and poet as preacher both, then, have a unique ability to promote, proclaim, and commence the production of a new reality.

The current reality faced by Phillis Wheatley and her enslaved contemporaries is primarily bodily. The poet-theologian seeks to articulate a new reality that is inspirational for the enslaved and compelling for the white reader. As a rhetor-poet-preacher, Wheatley poetically articulates "[t]he fight for control of the [black] body" to bring to the fore that which had been invisible. Granted, the black body had been seen, but only as a commodity.[26] Wheatley writes the black body into existence by flipping her society and "inherited" culture—her world—on its axis. She knows she must "turn the moral world upside down" to create a land of opportunity within a land of oppression with hopes of that new land and new vision replacing the current reality.[27] Through her poetic prophecy, particularly in works like "On Imagination" and "On Being Brought from Africa to America," Wheatley inverts the theological conversation by changing the back door to the front door. Echoes of the Deuteronomistic prophet rings throughout her poetry by her repositioning of the black body, even theoretically so, "And the Lord shall make thee the head, and not the tail; and thou shalt be above only, and thou shalt not be beneath."[28] Approaching, accessing, and articulating the self from the underside or back door of humanity is actually the appropriate stance for the committed theologian who desires to make claims about God and God's activity with and among creation.

Wheatley joins in this articulation of personhood thereby uniting her with prophets before her and those yet to come. By upending accepted mythologies of whiteness, such as the curse of Cain and the Hamatic myth, she works to de-otherize blacks in America. She reaches beyond their perceived non-citizenry in America to articulate in a fresh way the universal citizenry of the black body. She seeks to highlight the possibility of "a new world by transcending the narrow confines of the one in which [her people are] forced to live."[29] As Lawrence Levine has suggested, the desire of the preacher-as-creator is to extend "the boundaries of their restrictive universe backward until it fused with the world of the Old Testament, and upward until it became one with the world beyond."[30] This process of becoming gives precedence to freedom as necessary for a progressive movement. The challenge, however, is that this freedom cannot be mutually exclusive in any way. As a poetic prophet, Wheatley dislodges freedom's qualifiers out of the dominant culture's stable to reorder the dominant authoritative discourse.

AMID SUCH RESISTANCE, ONE HEARS CLEARLY THE PSALMIST DECLARING:

By the rivers of Babylon, there we sat down, yea, we wept, when we remembered Zion.

We hanged our harps upon the willows in the midst thereof.

For there they that carried us away captive required of us a song; and they that wasted us required of us mirth, saying, Sing us one of the songs of Zion.

How shall we sing the Lord's song in a strange land?

If I forget thee, O Jerusalem, let my right hand forget her cunning.

If I do not remember thee, let my tongue cleave to the roof of my mouth; if I prefer not Jerusalem above my chief joy.

Remember, O Lord, the children of Edom in the day of Jerusalem; who said, Rase it, rase it, even to the foundation thereof.

O daughter of Babylon, who art to be destroyed; happy shall he be, that rewardeth thee as thou hast served us.

Happy shall he be, that taketh and dasheth thy little ones against the stones.[31]

Here, the psalmist is recounting and recasting their current reality. There is both an understanding of the situation and an upheaval and desired dislodging of the current dominant paradigm of placed personhood. Preacher and writer, Frederick Douglass incorporates this psalm in his speech "What to the Slave Is the Fourth of July?" noting, "This Fourth [of] July is *yours*, not *mine*. *You* may rejoice, *I* must mourn. To drag a man in fetters into the grand illuminated temple of liberty, and call upon him to join you in joyous anthems, were inhuman mockery and sacrilegious irony."[32] He then continues to admonish his predominantly white audience stating, "It is dangerous to copy the example of a nation whose crimes, lowering up to heaven, were thrown down by the breath of the Almighty, burying that nation in irrecoverable ruin!"[33] In this moment, Douglass adopts the cry and lament of the psalmist paying particular attention to the need for preserving collective memory for the sake of progress and true freedom. In the midst of a burgeoning American empire, Douglass warns them of the dangers of becoming the next Babylon. He hears "the mournful wail of millions . . . whose chains, heavy and grievous yesterday, are, to-day, rendered more intolerable by the jubilee shouts that reach them."[34] Douglass believes his charge is to see America from the "slave's point of view," a stance or perspective that has consistently been overlooked and unappreciated. Within this psalm, the singers are not concerned with their location per se; rather, they are concerned about whether or not God is respected as "ruler" in the land.[35] It is the unbridled, reckless approach to governance and ultimately interpersonal interactions that needs to be checked. It is the job of the psalmist, the preacher, the prophet, and the poet to articulate this lament, plea, and prescription in a way that is digestible for the hearer/reader. Douglass, following Wheatley's lead, when given the platform to speak baits the audience with resounding, relatable rhetoric at the outset leading to a desired and designed prophetic turn.

Monescalchi argues that "Wheatley's seemingly inconsistent stance on slavery can be clarified once one takes her seriously as a theological thinker and recognizes that her conception of benevolence—especially one's obligation to exhibit benevolence in the face of human suffering—changed over time."[36] My contention is that politics and theology are inextricably linked due to the fact that a person's theology is developed through a coalescence of a person's knowledge about God coupled with their experience of God. I agree with him that Wheatley's theology evolves over time (as does everyone's). In addition, her individual poems are part of a whole, hence the collection *Poems on Various Subjects, Religious and Moral*. I do not believe Wheatley was disinterested in slavery in a detached way in her early poems, as Monescalchi purports; rather, I believe she is consistently committed to the cause of the liberation of her people throughout her poetry, yet it is expressed differently in each piece. As scholars, we make the choice as to how we choose to engage a particular writer and their works. It is clear that Monescalchi chooses to read Wheatley in a critical way that is genuine to her religious affiliations and social connections, while also maintaining a connection to Rev. Samuel Hopkins and his theological evolution. As mentioned, this is meaningful to understand more fully Wheatley's religious affiliations and the nuances of her social connections. It also helps with the overall mapping of her theological and voice development. The real question, however, is whether or not Wheatley is the chicken or the egg. It seems Monescalchi also wrestles with this query, noting: Given that Wheatley theorized her own version of disinterested benevolence in her Poems and used it to critique slavery before Hopkins—who corresponded with Wheatley and purchased "the largest known order for her book"[37]—did the same, this article argues that Wheatley influenced as much as she adhered to Hopkins's "New Divinity" brand of evangelicalism.[38]

The question that arises is did Hopkins actually use some of the theory and theology espoused in Wheatley's poetry to inform his formalized theological position, naming it "disinterested benevolence?" If Hopkins did inherit his evolved theology from Wheatley, then disinterested benevolence is more than likely an African spiritual principle that Wheatley knew of (and now had a new language for) and promoted throughout her poetry. As Hopkins notes, disinterested benevolence is a matter of vacating the individual will in order to take on the burden of caring for humanity. It is important to note that the requirement is to vacate the individual will but not the individual's status. Wheatley could not control her status, but she could control her will. It is a

Africentric way of being in the world, to choose to see other's problems as your own and vice versa. It is the process of living into your sister or brother's experience. It is in essence the Zulu principle of Ubuntu or "humanity towards others" that drives Wheatley in her writing. As Monescalchi rightly suggests, "Wheatley's evangelical theory of benevolence strategically permitted her to sustain her selfless condition and thus critique slavery without having to detail her own pain."[39] Wheatley's pain is detailed in the experiences of those Africans she refers to in her poetic verses. Additionally, Hopkins did not begin moving away from his equating slavery to an "advantageous sin" until 1770 when he moved to Newport, Rhode Island, and encountered slavery firsthand. By then, Wheatley had already begun writing and was somewhat known in New England. It is Wheatley, then, who introduces Hopkins to this concept. Hopkins, having the status, position, and influence, is then able to bring it to a larger audience in a more direct, palatable, and formalized way.

Wheatley's articulation of personhood emanates from a place of collective lament. It is from here that she is empowered or endowed with a third sight that inspires the shape of the words she pens. The poet-theologian, in this sense, has the ability to tap into "the linguistic spaces to bring the community to the point of recognition" of the possibility of a new reality in which people can "maintain their dignity and humanity in inhumane situations," thereby singing the Lord's song in a strange or inhumane land.[40] This third sight is provided from without. Some would call it inspiration. Inspiration, by definition, can emerge from within or from the outside. It is my suggestion that the poet-preacher is dually inspired. Being inspired from within, the poet-preacher is able to articulate the collective lament of her people; the internal resonance can be felt in the words written or articulated. Simultaneously, there is an external inspiration. This "curiosity" serves as the driving external force that strengthens the language with a nonmaterial quality. The outside inspiration becomes internalized by the poet-preacher. Articulation of a third sight requires the poet-preacher embody "the Aristotelian notion of poet as creator and receiver. . . . As a result[,] . . . the preacher stands in the prophetic tradition . . . receiv[ing] a vision from God [or the Muses] and communicat[ing] it hesitantly."[41] The new reality, then, emerges from the poet's willingness to be used while in creative mode. She becomes a vehicle for the transportation or delivery of a new message. She must take advantage of each opportunity to interrupt the status quo with a transgressive message for both a hurting people and, conversely, a savagely inhumane people. In order for this radical message to have lasting effect, there must be a radical recasting of the narrative by way of composing a type of poetic metanarrative of resilience and cultural consistency.

The cry of the committed carrier of the logos, the word of God, is convicting and convincing because the cry is both collaborative and representative.

Preachers "speak as members of a body and not for [themselves] alone, which means that [she] may not dominate the sermon any more than [she] may be absent from it."[42] Significantly, the preacher represents a particular community and articulates often an alternative narrative that stems from both collective witness and an internal conviction of compulsion. It is here the interplay among the poet-preacher, the people, and God is most clearly represented. As intimated by Alan of Lile, the poet-preacher must be able to relate to her audience "through the humility [she] shows . . . , and through the profitableness of [her] subject matter. [She] must say that [she] propounds the word of God to [her] listeners so that it may bring forth fruit in their minds, not for any earthly gain, but to set them on their way and to help them make progress."[43] Everything articulated by the poet-preacher should, at its best, bend toward "the edification of the listener."[44] It is vitally important to edify and equip the audience because they are the representatives of a fallen humanity. Particularly, within American history and culture, there is clear evidence of humanity's fallen state.

James Cone notes, rightly, that racism is "America's original sin and as it is institutionalized at all levels of society; it is its most persistent and intractable evil. Though racism inflicts massive suffering, few American theologians have even bothered to address white supremacy as a moral evil and as a radical contradiction of our humanity and religious identities."[45] This sin, represented by persistent acts of evil, becomes ensconced in the very fabric of American culture. It reaches beyond the plantation, to the town center, to the marketplace, to the urban centers of the north, and beyond. It is carried within the hearts, intentionally or not, of every white citizen. It is a worldview; therefore, it travels. Much like the religious oppression "escaped" by the Puritans, it is only a matter of time before that sentiment and mentality is reified in America. Since this original sin has been institutionalized, particularly through the slavocracy, there is a need for a righteous retaliation. This retaliation emerges through the precise rhetoric of the preacher. Wheatley, as poet-preacher, fills this role by combating the institutionalized moral evil. As Peter Paris has suggested, there is not an urging or impetus from within the "institution" of slavery to escape the clutches of sin. This sinful way of life is stoked and reinforced throughout the society on plantations, in town centers, in marketplaces, and in some urban centers. Even within the white church, this original sin is affirmed:

> White churches actually experienced no alienation between their thought and practice. This is evidenced by the fact that any attempt to preach racial equality in the pulpit has always been viewed as an act of hostility against the prevailing ethos. Since blacks assumed a static theology that transcended both races, they inevitably concluded that racist activities were deliberate violations of

professed theological beliefs. They had forgotten that the Christian churches ostensibly had no difficulty with slavery for centuries prior to the abolitionism of the nineteenth century. In fact, it is highly doubtful that the New Testament itself offers unequivocal opposition to slavery. Thus, if slavery had such a long history among Christians, one should not suppose that Christians would necessarily believe themselves to be under religious obligation to treat ex-slaves as first-class citizens.[46]

For these reasons, the poet-preacher is needed to cast an alternative theological vision for humanity.

Dolan Hubbard intimates that Hortense Spillers notes that "the preacher through his ritual form of expression—the sermon—sings the song of 'a Fallen man.' . . . [T]he metaphor of the fallen man . . . permeates black American culture . . . [and] celebrates heroic overcoming and achievement."[47] The idea of the preacher enjoining the trope of the fallen man is significant, particularly as it relates to the mandate of the preacher to speak for or on the behalf of the audience or community. Noting that Spillers's "Mama's Baby, Papa's Maybe" offers an analysis of the "theological underpinning of slavery and early modern colonialism," J. Kameron Carter analyzes the "operations of religion within the age of conquest."[48] There is a twofold fallenness that is apparent when engaging Spillers's works: fallen state as being in sin for whites and a being in limbo for blacks. Within this tension, "the preacher articulates the complicated relationship in America between historical memory and the American Dream."[49] The American Dream looms large for blacks in America, yet the reality of historical memory cannot be denied. The white American has access and often lives within the American Dream because of a racially skewed historical narrative. This narrative colors the tapestry of the American ideal white. To maintain this coloring of the social order, blacks in America must remain outside the lines. There is no room for blackness within a purely and decidedly white tapestry. So, the historical narrative from the white perspective, though dismissive of blacks as people, is built upon the slavocracy. Hence, the preacher is called to preach both a liberative word and a, simultaneously, redemptive word. The word of liberation comes to those black bodies who have "known rivers" of slave quarters, slave ships, the auction block, chains, whips, and phallic conquests. As Langston Hughes has eloquently articulated, the black body subjected to the intentional coloring of history by whites in America is not completely detached from her story:

> I've known rivers:
> I've known rivers ancient as the world and older than the flow of human blood in human veins.
>
> My soul has grown deep like the rivers.

> I bathed in the Euphrates when dawns were young.
> I built my hut near the Congo and it lulled me to sleep.
> I looked upon the Nile and raised the pyramids above it.
> I heard the singing of the Mississippi when Abe Lincoln went down to New Orleans, and I've seen its muddy bosom turn all golden in the sunset.
>
> I've known rivers:
> Ancient, dusky rivers.
>
> My soul has grown deep like the rivers.[50]

As with the poet, the preacher's rhetoric helps pull the current and former chattel out of a state of social limbo in which the American Dream simply hovers above as an empty promise. The word of redemption comes to those often privileged and always blinded white shells of humanity who are soulless. The shell, from creation, is filled with the breath of God; however, free will offers us every opportunity to rid ourselves of the essence of God within us.[51] These shells represent Fallen man. Hence, there is a need for redemption. It is a reclamation of sorts in which God refills the shell with a new soul. The challenge lies in the choice—free will. Just as whites in America freely chose to enslave Africans and choose to place barriers between them and the other, white Americans must freely choose to receive redemption. The preacher offers it, artistically so, yet the hearer must receive it and act on it. This is the challenge of redemption as overcoming and achievement.

P. T. Forsyth notes that he appreciates both the orator and the preacher, but he also expresses the clearly demarcated difference between the two:

> It is one thing to have to rouse or persuade people to do something; it is another to have to induce them to trust somebody and renounce themselves for him. The one is the political region of work, the other is the religious region of faith. . . . The orator, speaking generally, has for his business to make real and urgent the present world and its crises, the preacher a world unseen, and the whole crisis of the two worlds. . . . [The orator] may speak of affairs, of nature, or of imagination. In the pulpit he may be what is called a practical preacher, or a poet-preacher.[52]

The poet-preacher is uniquely gifted to inspire and invite. The inspiration points toward institution outward change. The invitation ignites an inward change—redemption. This dual process or work performed by the poet-preacher is pivotal for humanity's becoming.

The dual calling of the poet-preacher is significant, for the invitation and inspiration point toward a need to live into the very best of human dignity and potential. In her best-selling inspirational memoir, Michelle Obama intimates that "becoming isn't about arriving somewhere or achieving a certain aim. I see it instead as forward motion, a means of evolving, a way to reach continuously toward a better self. The journey doesn't end."[53] The poet-preacher knows both the importance of the journey and the lasting impression on the community from journeying well. The poet-preacher stands as a gatekeeper of sorts, making articulations that usher hearers into fertile transformation ground. Again, the clarion call of the poet-preacher is one of invitation and inspiration:

> Let's invite one another in. Maybe then we can begin to fear less, to make fewer wrong assumptions, to let go of the biases and stereotypes that unnecessarily divide us. Maybe we can better embrace the ways we are the same. . . . There's power in allowing yourself to be known and heard, in owning your unique story, in using your authentic voice. And there's grace in being willing to know and hear others. This . . . is how we become.[54]

Wheatley, as poet-preacher, remains engaged in this dual art of facilitating the process of becoming through her inspiration and invitation to create a better America. She articulates from the platform of the not yet to people living within a "maybe" reality, as expressed by Obama, who possess the courage to embrace the equality of humanity for the sake of the future of America.

The doctrine of creation is often articulated through the performance of the poet-preacher who "critiques the metaphorical system in which both the blackness of the corporate community and its experiences have been valorized by the dominant culture as a 'natural' absence from the historical realm."[55] The poet-preacher's sermon must be understood as an "interjection," which challenges the master narrative.[56] The interjection carries with it words of reassurance couched within the rhetoric of liberation while simultaneously invoking a re-creative invitation for salvation. The poet-preacher reassures the "despised community" that they represent a unique expression of the imago dei, a religio-political plea, while subversively presenting the "sublime subject" of the salvific work of Calvary and the cross that transcends temporal reality.[57]

There is value in the voice of the poet-preacher. The rhetoric sagaciously uncovers and presents "the gospel of One who condemns and challenges and converts. It is the purpose of God not to stamp out and obliterate the kingdoms of this world"; rather, these kingdoms "are to be redeemed."[58] Even America, says the committed poet-preacher, is eligible for redemption through re-creation.

Again, at the intersection of the sacred and the secular, the poet-preacher utters an invitational and inspirational word. Wheatley lives into this tradition by maintaining/retaining her Senegambian roots while conjuring the essence of the Christian tradition. As Charles H. Long suggests, meaning does not merely exist within a religious vacuum for the African American. Rather, within the tension-filled space, with the music, the folktales, and the incantations on the one hand and the formation of the American Christian church on the other, a unique type of dunamis emerges. It is a "great critical and creative power" that influences the "deeper religious issues regarding the true situation of black communities," pointing toward liberation.[59] Wheatley effectively uses this power to speak to the deeper issues of the black community, and she also uses this power to condemn, challenge, and convert the dominant culture. As poet-preacher, Wheatley uses her words to "transform historical consciousness into art," using that artistic expression to present a new iteration of both the black self and the white self. By simultaneously lifting the black community and challenging the white community, Wheatley effectively lives into her divine gifting, using/incorporating her scholarship, theological insights, style, and voice to re-create America.[60]

NOTES

1. Stone and Duke, *How to Think Theologically*, 2.
2. In Paul Tillich's *Theology of Culture*, he suggests, "Religion is being ultimately concerned about that which is and should be our ultimate concern" (40). Religion must be viewed in conjunction with culture and vice versa. Religion is superfluous and aimless without culture, and culture is malnourished without religion. Tillich further argues that "every religious act . . . is culturally formed" (42). Identity ceases to exist outside of a cultural expression, and that expression is the manifestation of wrestling with some ultimate concern.
3. Stone and Duke, 3.
4. Brueggemann, *The Prophetic Imagination*, 22.
5. Brueggemann, 22.
6. Wheatley, *Poems on Various Subjects*, 8.
7. Wheatley, 8.
8. Lischer, *The End of Words*, ix. Here, Lischer is quoting T. S. Eliot's *Four Quartets*.
9. Lischer, 5.
10. Lischer, 5.
11. Lischer, 6.
12. Baker, *Journey Back*, 31.
13. Baker, 31.
14. Baker, 31.
15. Deleuze and von Sacher-Masoch, *Masochism*, 33.
16. Castiglia, "Revolution Is a Fiction," 406.
17. Hubbard, *The Sermon and the African American Literary Imagination*, 24.

18. Hubbard, 13.
19. Spillers, "Fabrics of History: Essays on the Black Sermon," PhD diss., Brandeis University, 1974, 2, quoted in Dolan Hubbard, *The Sermon and the African American Literary Imagination*, 41.
20. Hubbard, 7.
21. King, *Strength to Love*, xiv.
22. Hubbard, 6.
23. Hubbard, 6.
24. Spillers, "Fabrics of History," 4, quoted in Dolan Hubbard, *The Sermon*, 41.
25. Emerson, "The Poet," 556.
26. Hubbard, 2.
27. Hubbard, 3.
28. Deut. 28:13 (KJV).
29. Levine, *Black Culture and Black Consciousness*, 32.
30. Levine, 33.
31. Ps. 137 (KJV).
32. Douglass, "What to the Slave Is the Fourth of July," 116.
33. Douglass, 116.
34. Douglass, 116.
35. Mays, *Psalms*, 423.
36. Monescalchi, "Rise of the Disinterested Benevolence," 415.
37. Grimsted, "Anglo American Racism," 372.
38. Monescalchi, 417.
39. Monescalchi, 416.
40. Hubbard, 7.
41. Hubbard, 17.
42. Taylor, *How Shall They Preach*, 84.
43. Lischer, 6.
44. Lischer, 7.
45. Cone, "Theology's Great Sin," 145.
46. Paris, *The Social Teaching of the Black Churches*, 76.
47. Hubbard, 76.
48. Carter, "Paratheological Blackness," 592. Carter's analysis is dependent upon a progressive reading of Spillers's notion of the ungendering of black people in chattel slavery. This, too, affords a more progressive reading of Hubbard, specifically noting the fallenness of man and the depreciation of value as a result. There is a connection between the fallen man and the commodification of human laborers—chattel. Personality is dismissed and property politics triumph, resulting in an unforgiving slavocracy which becomes the breeding ground for communal sin and eternal fallenness. The ensuing "overcoming and achievement" intimated by Hubbard is reliant upon the poet-preacher who is uniquely qualified to speak of the sacred within the confines of the secular.
49. Hubbard, 14.
50. Hughes, "The Negro Speaks of Rivers," 23.
51. See Gen. 1–2 (KJV).

52. Forsyth, "The Authority of the Preacher," 99.
53. Obama, *Becoming*, 419.
54. Obama, 421.
55. Hubbard,13.
56. Hubbard, 13.
57. Hubbard, 12–13.
58. Taylor, 109.
59. Long, *Significations*, 7.
60. See Horace Bushnell, "Pulpit Talent," 83–89.

Chapter 2

Encountering God through the Preacher

Wheatley's Influences

To the Rev. Dr. Thomas Amory on Reading His Sermons on Daily Devotion, in Which That Duty Is Recommended and Assisted

    TO cultivate in ev'ry noble mind
    Habitual grace, and sentiments refin'd,
    Thus while you strive to mend the human heart,
    Thus while the heav'nly precepts you impart,
    O may each bosom catch the sacred fire,   5
    And youthful minds to Virtue's throne aspire!

    When God's eternal ways you set in sight,
    And Virtue shines in all her native light,
    In vain would Vice her works in night conceal,
    For Wisdom's eye pervades the sable veil. 10

    Artists may paint the sun's effulgent rays,
    But Amory's pen the brighter God displays:
    While his great works in Amory's pages shine,
    And while he proves his essence all divine,
    The Atheist sure no more can boast aloud   15
    Of chance, or nature, and exclude the God;
    As if the clay without the potter's aid
    Should rise in various forms, and shapes self-made,
    Or worlds above with orb o'er orb profound
    Self-mov'd could run the everlasting round.   20
    It cannot be—unerring Wisdom guides
    With eye propitious, and o'er all presides.

    Still prosper, Amory! still may'st thou receive

> The warmest blessings which a muse can give,
> And when this transitory state is o'er,   25
> When kingdoms fall, and fleeting Fame's no more,
> May Amory triumph in immortal fame,
> A nobler title, and superior name![1]

THE INFLUENCE OF REV. DR. THOMAS ARMORY

It is through the imaginative act of creation that Wheatley articulates the possibility of a new reality for black people in America; her initial engagement and familiarity with the doctrine of creation is primarily inspired by ministers and revivalists she encounters such as George Whitefield, Joseph Sewall, and Thomas Amory. In particular, Thomas Amory seems to have inspired her intense interest in using creation mythology to advocate freedom. The poem "To Rev. Dr. Thomas Amory on Reading His Sermons on Daily Devotion, in Which That Duty Is Recommended and Assisted" is rarely critically engaged with the exception of passing observations, as in the case with Levernier, who uses four lines from the poem to argue that "morality for Wheatley is usually quite ambiguous."[2] He then returns to his analysis of "On Being Brought from Africa to America" without ever really engaging the quoted lines from "To the Rev. Dr. Thomas Armory." A closer reading of the poem, particularly lines 11–22, however, reveals Wheatley's defense of the doctrine of divine creation as a significant and indispensable component of the human experience and portrays the creator God as the ultimate guide for a fulfilled life.

> Artists may paint the sun's effulgent rays,
> But *Amory's* pen the brighter God displays:
> While his great works in *Amory's* pages shine,
> And while he proves his essence all divine,
> The Atheist sure no more can boast aloud
> Of chance, or nature, and exclude the God;
> As if the clay without the potter's aid
> Should rise in various forms, and shapes self-made,
> Or worlds above with orb o'er orb profound
> Self-mov'd could run the everlasting round.
> It cannot be—unerring *Wisdom* guides
> With eye propitious, and o'er all presides.[3]

Immediately, the reader familiar with Wheatley remembers her invocation of Homer and his artistic prowess in "To Maecenas" and her assessment of him as one who captured the created image of God—humankind. Similarly, as she continues to praise Amory's sophistication and proficiency, she notes that he promotes the creative works of God that prove the particular Creator's divinity, "all divine."[4] Wheatley is noting a stark contrast between humanity and divinity. The obvious argument is that God is divine and humans are not as she presents her defense, which supports the sufficiency of divine creation. In lines 15–22, Wheatley presents a strong categorical defense of divine creation, challenging the atheist's ability to deny God. She disavows chance and nature as agents of creation, noting the necessity of God in the creative act. What the atheist and others consider "chance" or "nature" are extensions of the creative act or processes within the creative act. Her use of imagery is significant here, likening God to a potter and humans to clay. This is undoubtedly a reference to the narrative of the potter in Jeremiah 18 where the prophet Jeremiah is instructed to go to the potter's house. He observes, "Behold, [the potter] wrought a work on the wheels. And the vessel that he made of clay was marred in the hand of the potter: so he made it again another vessel, as seemed good to the potter to make it."[5] Just as the clay shaped by the potter in the biblical account is imperfect yet "reworked" into perfection, the human clay in this world must be shaped and reshaped by the divine potter. Here, Wheatley makes the case that if God's greatest creation is human beings, all of humankind is entitled to full liberation. By virtue of the potter's mind imagining and the potter's hands shaping the clay, there is some divinity within humanity. The imagery of the potter and clay serves as an illustrative recapitulation of the creation narrative in Genesis in which God, the potter, shaped humankind "in our image, according to our likeness" and breathed the breath of life into the physical body of humankind.[6] The pure breath from God represents the essence of the spirit, divinity, in its purest form. The created being or clay represents the rawness of human nature.

Wheatley further illustrates the relationship between God and humanity in lines 17 through 20, "As if clay without the potter's aid / Should rise in various forms, and shapes self-made, / Or worlds above with orb o'er orb profound / Self-mov'd could run the everlasting round."[7] For Wheatley, creation, articulated in line 18 as rising and formation, is neither self-initiated nor a chance occurrence. Regardless of the "forms" or "shapes" individuals take, in terms of race or gender, all possess the same apportionment of divinity and have been carefully crafted by the potter. She further argues that the "profound" celestial space is also created by God and must be earnestly taken into consideration. For these reasons, Wheatley notes that the race or "round" of life is lacking or incomplete without the guided or directed movements of God. All probable success in life and for humanity is directly connected to the omnipotence of God alone. Humans, therefore, are not to treat others as unequal nor to interfere with God's plan for his creation. In Wheatley's time, the white slaveholders had in effect assumed the role of the potter to create their own social order. Wheatley attempts to present a potential transformational process for their return to God's original plan; this process is only understood through a proper understanding of the doctrine of creation—thus emerges her theory of salvation.

Wheatley reads salvation as a transformational path to liberate all people from darkness. While most theologians and preachers view(ed) salvation as redemption from sin, bringing about new life for the unbeliever, Wheatley expands this view by suggesting salvation is only the beginning of a transformative process that requires the ongoing and continuous refining of self that leads to change and improvement. The change and improvement comes from belief being applied to action. She seems to suggest that people are "by works . . . justified, and not by faith only."[8] Wheatley admonishes slave and slave-owner alike to allow their faith to motivate their actions to create a changed or transformed society, one that is more in line with God's idea of humanity—where all are equal and divinely made.

On the Death of the Rev. Mr. George Whitefield. 1770

HAIL, happy saint, on thine immortal throne,
Possest of glory, life, and bliss unknown;
We hear no more the music of thy tongue,
Thy wonted auditories cease to throng.
Thy sermons in unequall'd accents flow'd, 5
And ev'ry bosom with devotion glow'd;
Thou didst in strains of eloquence refin'd

Inflame the heart, and captivate the mind.
Unhappy we the setting sun deplore,
So glorious once, but ah! it shines no more. 10

Behold the prophet in his tow'ring flight!
He leaves the earth for heav'n's unmeasur'd height,
And worlds unknown receive him from our sight.
There Whitefield wings with rapid course his way,
And sails to Zion through vast seas of day. 15
Thy pray'rs, great saint, and thine incessant cries
Have pierc'd the bosom of thy native skies.
Thou moon hast seen, and all the stars of light,
How he has wrestled with his God by night.
He pray'd that grace in ev'ry heart might dwell, 20
He long'd to see America excel;
He charg'd its youth that ev'ry grace divine
Should with full lustre in their conduct shine;

That Saviour, which his soul did first receive,
The greatest gift that ev'n a God can give, 25
He freely offer'd to the num'rous throng,
That on his lips with list'ning pleasure hung.

"Take him, ye wretched, for your only good,
Take him ye starving sinners, for your food;
Ye thirsty, come to this life-giving stream, 30
Ye preachers, take him for your joyful theme;
Take him my dear Americans, he said,
Be your complaints on his kind bosom laid:
Take him, ye Africans, he longs for you,
"Impartial Saviour is his title due: 35
Wash'd in the fountain of redeeming blood,
You shall be sons, and kings, and priests to God."

Great Countess, 1 we Americans revere
Thy name, and mingle in thy grief sincere;
New England deeply feels, the Orphans mourn, 40
Their more than father will no more return.

But, though arrested by the hand of death,
Whitefield no more exerts his lab'ring breath,
Yet let us view him in th' eternal skies,
Let ev'ry heart to this bright vision rise; 45
While the tomb safe retains its sacred trust,
Till life divine re-animates his dust.[9]

The Influence of Rev. Mr. George Whitefield

Wheatley provides the genesis for the reframing of concepts in Christian theology, particularly salvation, and she appropriates the Cain narrative to enhance, extend, and re-envision our conceptualization of mercy. Wheatley argues for a radical salvation that is simultaneously Adventist and Pentecostal, not in a denominational sense but in the understanding of the distinct definitions of the repetitive terms. Advent celebrates the arrival of God through Christ to do for us what we could not do for ourselves. This promise of a savior is important for the Negroes Wheatley seeks to encourage. Pentecost, on the other hand, celebrates the arrival of God through the Spirit to reconstitute how we experience worship and how we see others, resulting in how we treat others. Belief alters perception to transform actions or works. This promise is significant for the white people Wheatley engages, for they must see the people within their communities differently. Salvation, as depicted by Wheatley then, is both a new birth and a radical call to progress, and the belief that salvation is available for sinners and saints alike would have been a novel view of salvation for her time because saints do not need salvation.

Wheatley expands her understanding of the democratic nature of salvation and its transformative potential through her articulation of grace in "On the Death of Rev. Mr. George Whitefield." In other words, Wheatley gives voice to a universalized understanding of salvation and its transformative potential. She articulates a nondiscriminatory soteriology. The grace extended to all by the "Impartial Saviour" is necessary for communal success and cultural advancement. In her poetic eulogy Wheatley states:

> He pray'd that grace in ev'ry heart might dwell,
> He long'd to see *America* excel;
> He charg'd its youth that ev'ry grace divine
> Should with full lustre in their conduct shine;
> That Saviour, which his soul did first receive,
> The greatest gift that even a God can give,
> He freely offer'd to the num'rous throng,
> That on his lips with list'ning pleasure hung.
> "Take him, ye wretched, for your only good,
> "Take him ye starving sinners, for your food;
> "Ye thirsty, come to this life-giving stream,
> "Ye preachers, take him for your joyful theme;
> "Take him my dear *Americans*, he said,
> "Be your complaints on his kind bosom laid:
> "Take him, ye *Africans*, he longs for you,
> "*Impartial Saviour* is his title due:
> "Wash'd in the fountain of redeeming blood,
> "You shall be sons, and kings, and priests to God."[10]

Whitefield's prayer that grace might dwell in every heart correlates well with Wheatley's articulation of a dual/democratic salvation. Grace, God's unmerited favor toward man made possible by Jesus's death, is extended to all who will receive it. Consequently, salvation is an act of grace. Viewing salvation as grace, Wheatley disembarks from Calvinist leanings that espouse only certain people, "the Elect," are eligible to be saved.[11] Likewise, the Gospel evangelist John states, "For God so loved the world, that he gave his only begotten Son, that whosoever believeth in him should not perish, but have everlasting life."[12] John's use of "the world" and "whosoever" removes any true acceptance of a divine elect or the possession of divine right. The gift of salvation that is graciously extended by God does not require anything but acceptance. Wheatley, as a diligent student of the Bible, would have been familiar with John's gospel and its ecumenical appeal. Her desire (and Whitefield's) is that grace would be accepted by slave and free, black and white. Wheatley and Whitefield espouse if all of America realized they were recipients of God's grace, the result would be the emergence of a more perfect Christian world. This is not to suggest that all the enslaved and slavers had to do was accept the grace to make everything well. Rather, the acceptance of this grace is just the beginning of the process.

After establishing Whitefield's desire for America to excel morally and his understanding of salvation's role in attaining cultural improvement, Wheatley quotes Whitefield to emphasize the urgency with which the evangelist presented grace in preaching a gospel of love. Wheatley identifies three categories of individuals who are eligible to receive salvation through grace: the "wretched," the "sinners," and the "thirsty."[13] Hence, whether people are Christians or are unbelievers, as long as they fit into one of these three categories, they qualify to receive salvation. These categories are inclusive of black people and white people, enslaved and free. In line 28, the wretched represent those individuals who are promoters and protectors of evil in the world, so they must accept this extension of grace for their "only good." Likewise, the sinners must receive grace for their nourishment.[14] Sin directly correlates to separation and depravity. The grace extended works to bridge this chasm between man and God. Even Christians need to accept this grace to be consistently drawn to God. Wheatley's use of the term "thirsty" can be read one of two ways. Either the thirsty represent those who are longing for something to fulfill their lives, or the thirsty represents those who are Christians and recognize that the grace extended by God is in fact a "life-giving stream."[15] In John 19:28, Jesus says, "I thirst" while dying on the cross. Jesus's declaration of thirst is directly connected to Whitefield's life-giving stream. The gospel of John records, "But one of the soldiers with a spear pierced his side, and forthwith came there out blood and water."[16] Upon the piercing of his side, the "life-giving stream" began to flow. If the stream stops flowing, the possibility of redemption ceases as well. The coupling of thirst with the life-giving stream expresses both a desire of humankind to connect with God and a desire for humankind to be connected with each other. If Wheatley is referring to this last saying of Jesus, "I thirst," she is directly connecting the thirst of humanity with that of Jesus. Jesus's articulation of thirst is really a statement of recommitment to his initial vow of thirst when he tells his mother, "How is it that ye sought me? wist ye not that I must be about my Father's business?"[17] Being about his father's business or in his father's house is a place of resistance to separation from God principally. For Wheatley, the concept of thirst in line 30 suggests a need for consistent dwelling with God, which proves to be a significant desire of Jesus as well. It is his love of God and desire to be in God's house that compels him to love, which is the premise upon which grace is given. The wretched, sinner, and thirsty are capable of embodying this love. Wheatley's tripartite approach maintains the dualism of salvation expressed in "On Being Brought from Africa to America" yet pushes the dualism further to redefine the categories of "Christian" and "pagan." Again, she juxtaposes the African and American in lines 32 and 34 to suggest that God endears God's self to the enslaved and the free alike. However, God's desire for both groups is expressed through the Impartial Savior who embodies grace and grants equal access to the promise articulated through the presentation of those like Whitefield.

In the final instance, Wheatley suggests that after the acceptance of grace comes the experience of life under grace. Lines 36 through 37 explicitly note the consequence of accepting the *Impartial Saviour*: "Wash'd in the fountain of redeeming blood, / You shall be sons, and kings, and priests to God." Wheatley's use of "to" God defines the relationship and places man in a unified communal experience under grace wherein all serve God equally. By so doing, she emphasizes God's perspective as opposed to the human perspective of sonship, kingship, and priesthood. We are all sons, kings, and priests in God's eyes but not necessarily in others' eyes. So, by experiencing grace, we begin to see each other through the eyes of God. This is Wheatley's ultimate goal in presenting salvation through the grace which is extended by an impartial savior. Humankind serves God rather than man.

The idea of the impartial savior, which eventually is tied to the idea of escape in the poem, is significant and a key focus of much of the extant scholarship on "On the Death of Rev. Mr. George Whitefield." Davis notes that Wheatley uses four lines (as opposed to one or two for the other addressees) to address "ye Africans," and it is also at this juncture that she invokes the term impartial:

> "Take him, ye *Africans*, he longs for you,
> "*Impartial Saviour* is his title due:
> "Wash'd in the fountain of redeeming blood,
> "You shall be sons, and kings, and priests to God."[18]

He further notes, "All through this passage there runs the obvious theme of escape through leveling which was Christianity's primary appeal to the slave. . . . It was the only way for Africans to enter into the 'kingdom' both here and hereafter."[19] If the ultimate goal is escape for Wheatley, there would be no need for her approach, for she could simply talk about escape as opposed to redemption and restoration. Davis seems to focus on the poem in light of the enslaved African's physical status without any consideration for the enslaveds" or slaveholder's moral state. If the Savior Wheatley invokes is impartial, the import of the poetic verse must also be impartial and convey a theme other than escape. R. Lynn Matson seeks to expound on this theme of escape in Wheatley's poem by referencing an earlier version of the same four lines:

> "Take him, ye Africans he longs for you,
> "Impartial savior is his title due.
> "If you will walk in Grace's heavenly Road,
> "He'll make you free, and Kings, and priests to God."[20]

Matson suggests that perhaps Wheatley changed "He'll make you free," to "You shall be sons" so as not to be "too obvious" and "to protect herself."[21] Her assumption may be plausible and could help to explain why a writer might adjust her or his language while maintaining the same message. However, her analysis ends with the assumption without engaging the language of the text; hence, her argument parallels Davis's 1953 argument of variations of escape in multiple versions of the poem. Will Harris advances the comparative analysis in "Phillis Wheatley, Diaspora Subjectivity, and the African American Canon," noting that Wheatley "explicitly politicizes both Whitefield and the Christian message of salvation by emphasizing freedom and equality in Christ," not just salvation and divine right.[22] Harris's argument lends itself to a much broader exploration of complexity of Wheatley's message. The challenge with the "escape theme" is that neither version of the poem presents the individual, whether "wretched," "sinners," "preachers," "Americans," or "Africans," as the active party in the relationship. The individual simply must "take him," at which time the impartial Savior will wash each individual and make each one free. Since the impartial Savior is the liberating agent, the individual is merely a recipient of the freeing act. While critics like Davis and Matson identify an escape theme, it is also an illustration of an impartial pardon.

Harris recognizes Wheatley's politicization of salvation, but he does not articulate her goal. The impartial savior, as agent, serves as the vessel through which grace is extended. The acceptance of grace results in a transformed spirit, mind, and moral compass, which directly affects communal engagement. Hence, cultural improvement is possible. Though the argument that God is impartial is not new, Wheatley's identification of the Christian's need for acceptance of renewed salvation through grace is unique, particularly as articulated by a slave. Moreover, Davis and Matson's suggestion that Wheatley's articulation of salvation, "*Impartial Saviour* is his title due: / Wash'd in the fountain of redeeming blood, / You shall be sons, and kings, and priests to God,"[23] only applies to the Africans is problematic because it dismisses the requirement for all people to be redeemed. A more sophisticated literary interpretation examines the poet's style. In the lines quoted at the outset of this section, lines 20 through 37, there are three words that are italicized throughout, *America(ns), Africans,* and *Impartial Saviour.* This stylistic choice is interesting. My suggestion is that Wheatley italicizes these words to highlight the availability of salvation through the Impartial Savior to both the American and African. This assertion, on Wheatley's part, is significant because it is countercultural. The established belief is that divine right prevents salvation for the African. Wheatley is suggesting that salvation has always been available to the African just as it has always been available to the American. Now, both the African and American must be cleansed by the "redeeming blood."

Wheatley's poetics is dripping with this transformative blood as she articulates a new reality for her community. Her words carry with them compulsion and conviction, inspiration and instruction, adulation and recognition, frustration, and hopeful anticipation. Though not uttered from the pulpit or some lofty platform, her words amplify just the same.

NOTES

1. Wheatley, "To the Rev. Dr. Thomas Amory, on Reading His Sermons on Daily Devotion, in Which That Duty Is Recommended and Assisted," in *Poems on Various Subjects*, pp. 90–91, lines 1–28.
2. Levernier, "Style as Protest," 183.
3. Wheatley, "To the Rev. Dr. Thomas Armory," pp. 90–91, lines 11–22.
4. Wheatley, "To the Rev. Dr. Thomas Armory," p. 90, line 14.
5. Jer. 18:3b-4 (KJV).
6. Gen. 1:26a (KJV).
7. Wheatley, "To the Rev. Dr. Thomas Armory," p. 91, lines 17–20.
8. Jam. 2:24 (KJV).
9. Wheatley, "On the Death of the Rev. Mr. George Whitefield. 1770" in *Poems on Various Subjects*, pp. 22–24, lines 1–47.
10. Wheatley, "On the Death of Rev. Mr. George Whitefield," p. 23, lines 20–37.
11. In the mid-eighteenth century, particularly during the first Great Awakening, Calvinist doctrine proved influential with revivalists such as Jonathan Edwards, who used it to frame his theology. Within the Calvinistic tradition, there is no such thing as works righteousness; an individual cannot perform good deeds to gain eternal life. Rather, it is through God's election of you as a child of God that you are then compelled to act justly toward others aided by the abiding presence of the Holy Spirit. Under this theological rubric, all of humanity is not considered elect. The Elect, on the other hand, are chosen by God to inherit eternal life in addition to being the recipients of provisions while on earth. Wheatley presents a new lens for understanding identity politics within the American protestant tradition, one that exposes the limitations of Calvinist doctrine and expands the soteriological boundaries of Wesleyan thought. Historians have noted the commonalities within the theologies of the revivalists during the First Great Awakening; "Luminaries such as Jacob Frelinghuysen, Gilbert

Tennent, George Whitefield, and Jonathan Edwards . . . preached a series of revivals . . . that led to an increased number of people making professions of faith, a resurgence in Calvinism, a deepening of piety, and a greater concern for education" (Allison, *Historical Theology*, 746).

12. Jn 3:16 (KJV).
13. Wheatley, "On the Death of Rev. Mr. George Whitefield," p. 23, lines 28–30.
14. Wheatley, "On the Death of Rev. Mr. George Whitefield," p. 23, line 29.
15. Wheatley, "On the Death of Rev. Mr. George Whitefield," p. 23, line 30.
16. Jn 19:34 (KJV).
17. Lk 2:49 (KJV).
18. Wheatley, "On the Death of Rev. Mr. George Whitefield," p. 23, lines 34–37.
19. Davis, "Personal Elements," 194.
20. Wheatley, *The Poems of Phillis Wheatley*, 70, quoted in R. Lynn Matson, "Phillis Wheatley—Soul Sister?," 226.
21. Matson, "Phillis Wheatley—Soul Sister?," 226.
22. Harris, "Diaspora Subjectivity," 39.
23. Wheatley, "On the Death of Rev. Mr. George Whitefield," p. 23, lines 35–37.

Chapter 3

The Spoken Word
On Isaiah 63:1–8

Isaiah LXIII. 1–8

SAY, heav'nly muse, what king, or mighty God,
That moves sublime from Idumea's road?
In Bozrah's dies, with martial glories join'd,
His purple vesture waves upon the wind.
Why thus enrob'd delights he to appear   5
In the dread image of the Pow'r of war?

Compress'd in wrath the swelling wine-press groan'd,
It bled, and pour'd the gushing purple round.

"Mine was the act," th' Almighty Saviour said,
And shook the dazzling glories of his head,   10
"When all forsook I trod the press alone,
And conquer'd by omnipotence my own;
For man's release sustain'd the pond'rous load,
For man the wrath of an immortal God:
To execute th' Eternal's dread command   15
My soul I sacrific'd with willing hand;
Sinless I stood before the avenging frown,
Atoning thus for vices not my own."

His eye the ample field of battle round
Survey'd, but no created succours found;   20
His own omnipotence sustain'd the fight,
His vengeance sunk the haughty foes in night;
Beneath his feet the prostrate troops were spread,
And round him lay the dying, and the dead.

Great God, what light'ning flashes from thine eyes? 25
What pow'r withstands if thou indignant rise?

Against thy Zion though her foes may rage,

>And all their cunning, all their strength engage,
>Yet she serenely on thy bosom lies,
>Smiles at their arts, and all their force defies.¹   30

SCRIPTURE: Isaiah 63:1–8

63 Who is this that cometh from Edom, with dyed garments from Bozrah? this that is glorious in his apparel, travelling in the greatness of his strength? I that speak in righteousness, mighty to save.

² Wherefore art thou red in thine apparel, and thy garments like him that treadeth in the winefat?

³ I have trodden the winepress alone; and of the people there was none with me: for I will tread them in mine anger, and trample them in my fury; and their blood shall be sprinkled upon my garments, and I will stain all my raiment.

⁴ For the day of vengeance is in mine heart, and the year of my redeemed is come.

⁵ And I looked, and there was none to help; and I wondered that there was none to uphold: therefore mine own arm brought salvation unto me; and my fury, it upheld me.

⁶ And I will tread down the people in mine anger, and make them drunk in my fury, and I will bring down their strength to the earth.

⁷ I will mention the loving kindnesses of the Lord, and the praises of the Lord, according to all that the Lord hath bestowed on us, and the great goodness toward the house of Israel, which he hath bestowed on them according to his mercies, and according to the multitude of his lovingkindnesses.

⁸ For he said, Surely they are my people, children that will not lie: so he was their Saviour.²

Spoken word is an art form that has been around informally since the beginning of spoken language; however, it has seen a reemergence in the last thirty years. Spoken word as poetic art form is commonplace once again. Ironically, this form of poetic verse harkens back to the oral tradition of classical Africa. That tradition maintained that there were griots, or more accurately jali and jalimuso, who served as the protectors of the historical narrative.³ As Ayi Kwei Armah suggests, the griots and scribes of feudal Africa" used their skills and intellect to maintain the "existing world order."⁴ He goes on to state that he intends to use his skills to create a better world order. This mission to create a better world order seems to be in line with a certain iteration or conceptualization of the griot tradition. Armah records that a shift occurred within the griot tradition following the Berlin Conference of 1884–1885; "[b]ecause that conference gave the go-ahead to any European state capable of organizing sufficient violence to seize African territories, it was followed by a series of land-grabbing assaults on what remained of the old African feudal order after four centuries of European slave raiding and destruction."[5] The reality of the incessant pressure and persecution at the hands of Europeans proves disabling for many of the feudal societies in Africa. In this season, the same griots who intended to maintain the status quo reached beyond the reality of what had been and what was to a hopeful future not yet realized. Armah adds that there is something unique about

> the record left by those griots who chronicled the final defeat of their sovereigns. . . . African intellectuals educated under colonial rule were taught to see colonial conquest as a civilizing, developmental process—a gain. Griots in the post-Berlin decades had a different consciousness of what was happening. They saw the imposition of colonial rule as defeat—a historical and cultural loss. . . . The griots mourning the end of a vanishing order provide a more intelligent vision of Africa's situation. . . . [Namely,] loss and defeat were not, for them, unusual themes.[6]

These griots are doing more than merely maintaining the status quo of the existing world order. These griots are invoking the spirit of the Sankofa bird.[7] There is a need to reclaim the best of what is past while continuing forward to a brighter future. This mission is salvific in nature and bespeaks a people's resilience and simultaneous resistance.

In truth, this is the Africentric mission that is couched within the verses of Wheatley's poetry: resilience and resistance. In "Isaiah lxiii.1–8," Wheatley engages the Judeo-Christian prophetic tradition of reading *the Word* into an Old Testament passage of scripture.[8] This is a common practice within Jewish, Muslim, and Christian exegetical practices. For Jews, the prophets point to a messiah who is yet to come. Muslims hold that Jesus is God's uniquely chosen prophet of Islam who will return to judge the ad-dajjal (imposter or false prophet). Christians, likewise, agree the prophets point to a messiah who is yet to come; however, they hold that this messiah is represented in the historical Jesus of Nazareth who has come and was crucified but raised physically from the dead, taken back to heaven to be with his "Father" and will come again to bring judgment for the lost and new life for "believers." The idea is that God alludes to a savior who is the embodiment of resilience and resistance in the Old Testament to prepare a people to receive this savior or messiah in the New Testament. In the Gospel tradition, "In the beginning was the Word, and the Word was with God, and the Word was God," [9] suggests that this Messiah—the Word—was present prior to Creation and "the Word was made flesh, and dwelt among us, (and we beheld his glory, the glory as of the only begotten of the Father,) full of grace and truth."[10] This is the vantage point from which the self-proclaimed Christian reads scripture. For this reason, Wheatley captures this spoken Word in this poem. She sagaciously exposes the Word within the words of the revered Old Testament prophet Isaiah to point to a new American reality.

Stephen Prothero suggests that within America there is a Jesus figure who is "neither the 'living Christ' of faith nor the 'historical Jesus' of scholarship."[11] This figure or "Word" operates as a specter within American culture. Prothero continues that his quest in writing *American Jesus: How the Son of God Became a National Icon* is to uncover "the cultural Jesus, who belongs neither to ancient Palestine nor to Christian America but to all of us, Christians and non-Christians alike. . . . [He is] searching for the American Jesus—Jesus as he has been interpreted and reinterpreted, construed and misconstrued, in the messy midrash of American culture."[12] Echoing E. P. Sanders, in a sense, Prothero seems to suggest that there is a cultural practice of oversight, dismissal, and erasure within America as it pertains to Jesus of Nazareth. Sanders describes the scene:

> On a spring morning about the year 30 C.E., three men were executed by the Roman authorities in Judea. Two were "brigands" . . . the third was executed as another type of political criminal. He had not robbed, pillaged, murdered, or even stored arms. He was convicted, however, of have claimed to be "king of the Jews"—a political title. Those who looked on . . . doubtless thought that . . . the world would little note what happened that spring morning. . . . It turned out, of course, that the third man, Jesus of Nazareth, would become one of the most important figures in human history.[13]

This practice of erasure has resulted in an ability to claim certain aspects or attributes of Jesus that are politically and socially palatable while dismissing others. Arguably, this has plagued America since her inception. Yet, at pivotal junctures within her history and development, a modern-day prophet emerges to harken America back to her foundation—"one nation under God." Phillis Wheatley, through her artistic interpretation of the words of the prophet Isaiah lives into the prophetic tradition as a type of griot, reclaiming that which is essential, while pushing for a reconceptualized future that challenges, radically so, the status quo. Her indictment of the promoters of this prized American Jesus is presented through "Isaiah lxiii. 1–8." Through this poem, Wheatley unseats the American Jesus (the specter) to reclaim the Radical Christ (the Word).

It is fitting that Wheatley uses the prophet Isaiah to reclaim the radical Christ, for the book of Isaiah is considered one of the most detailed prophetic accounts of the coming Christ in canonized scripture. As is evidenced through Wheatley's representation of Isaiah, the prophet has and shared a unique experience with the God of Israel. Isaiah, like the poet, is a seer, and his contemporaries "needed to see what [he] saw regarding the condition of their society and the hypocrisy of their religion."[14] Isaiah articulates his longing for redemption and rescue for his people through his vision in chapter 63. Here, Isaiah sees someone in the distance coming toward him and asks very simply who it is. Wheatley, likewise, desires for Americans to see what she sees "regarding the condition of [American] society and the hypocrisy of [American] religion."[15]

Wheatley opens this poem requesting the inspiration of the heavenly muse. Much like the prophet Isaiah, Wheatley suggests that whatever resolution or recommendation that follows is not of her conjuring but, rather, is divinely inspired to present the Word in a unique way. The two-pronged question she posits mirrors that of the prophet. She initially asks, "What king, or mighty God, / That moves sublime from Idumea's road?"[16] She follows this question up with a leading question, "Why thus enrobed delights he to appear / In the dread image of the Pow'r of war?"[17] As she peers on the horizon, she sees a figure approaching and asks who it is, king or God, moving with such sublimity, clearly cloaked in the garments of war. Her use of the sublime is not without purpose.

Dolan Hubbard in his chapter "W.E.B. Du Bois and the Invention of the Sublime in *The Souls of Black Folk*" presents an argument promoting Du Bois as a philosopher offering his insight to the long-standing debate surrounding the parameters of the sublime. He calls for a "reevaluation of" the sublime—one in which blacks are not left out unable to gain access.[18] In many literary criticism circles, particularly in recent history, as I noted in the introduction, there is hot debate around aesthetics in eighteenth-century American Literature. I believe the foundation for these debates rests in this notion of the sublime or the quality within a work of art that strikes an aesthetic chord. For, aesthetics is concerned with the appreciation of the perceived beauty within art, but the sublime is the beauty. The committed reader of Wheatley criticism or student of American literature and history has undoubtedly encountered the framing quote prose of Thomas Jefferson who writes, "Religion, indeed, has produced a Phyllis Wheatley; but it could not produce a poet. The compositions published under her name are below the dignity of criticism."[19] Historically, or at least Euro-historically, blacks have been placed on the underside without consideration of artistic abilities and capabilities. Simply, blacks are incapable of producing anything that possesses true beauty as demarcated by a hegemonic definition of *reasoned art*.[20]

Cahill and Larkin have underscored,

> We take aesthetics . . . as that concerned with the range of meanings comprehended by the correspondence of *feeling* and *form* in social, political, cultural, and natural objects. That is, we assume that all forms are aesthetic insofar as

they have the potential to produce feelings in perceiving subjects (or if they have been produced by artists in response to such feelings). At the same time, we contend, all feelings are aesthetic if they emerge in response to forms (or lead to the production of such forms).[21]

This definition, broad as it may be, is significant when encountering Wheatley as prophetic poet because she is writing her reactions to her lived experience in poetic verse. Her poetry has been produced "in response to" her feelings. Inversely, her feelings "lead to the production" of poetic verse that engages her audience in aesthetic ways. They conclude their defining remarks by noting, "Aesthetics is defined not only by privilege but also by difference, not only by the status of the subject but also the nature of its experience; and the charge of the literary scholar is to analyze not so much a particular set of objects as a particular phenomenological process."[22] When Jefferson seeks to define the aesthetic worth of Wheatley's poetry, he is doing so out of the blindness of his privilege and elitism and an innate need to frame the other as less than for the sake of maintenance. This has long been a criticism of the aesthetic critique, that it is too subjective and preference-driven. Jefferson's blind spot is, in my estimation, the traditional Americanist blind spot. When literature, history, sociology, or a myriad of other disciplines are approached from a Eurocentric basis, there tends to emerge an inability by the practitioner to see the other.

The hermeneutical stance of the individual, then, serves as the genesis for uncovering or, in Hubbard's term, "inventing" the sublime. No evaluation or valuation is needed to invent the sublime. It emerges from the artist. The European notion of the sublime espouses sublimity as, in Rudolph Otto's terms, the "mysterium tremendum,"[23] which is experiential, yet unable to be experienced by blacks because of their deficient intellectual capabilities. Interestingly, hermeneutics relies on experience for understanding a thing; therefore, it is my estimation that Wheatley participates in the invocation of hermeneutics to invent the black or true sublime while simultaneously deconstructing the European articulation of the sublime uncovering the spirituality or engagement with the divine of black people as the foundation for beauty. This reality is antithetical to the European worldview that grounds the interpretive stances of the Jeffersonians because religion and philosophy cannot coincide; they must be sectioned off. The African sensibility, however, has traditionally involved an enmeshing of disciplines that all form the holistic narrative that is life. According to Hubbard, Du Bois uses hermeneutics as a point of departure because it is a primary methodology within religion, which is "inseparable from aesthetics, the sublime, and identity formation."[24]

Contextualizing the sublime and joining the conversation among Longinus, Kant, and Du Bois locates the point of departure for Hubbard at a troubling philosophical juncture. I will get to the discussion as to why it is troubling in a moment, but I believe a brief engagement with Longinus and Kant is necessary to appreciate what Du Bois and Wheatley are doing. Longinus, who would have been most influential during the eighteenth century, casts five significant sources of the sublime: grandeur of thought, vehement and inspired passion, elevated figures of speech, noble phrasing of diction, and elevation in the arrangement of words.[25] For Kant, the feeling of the sublime stirs something within the human mind that is not easily explained. He notes, "The very capacity of conceiving the sublime . . . indicates a mental faculty that far surpasses every standard of sense."[26] With regard to our standards for judgment as it relates to the sublime, "Kant points out that as we find ourselves compelled to postulate a sensus communis to account for the agreement of men in their appreciation of beautiful objects."[27] What then is discovered to buttress their consent or agreement in judging what is and what is not beautiful or sublime is actually "the presupposition of the moral feeling in man,"[28] meaning our judgments of the sublime are connected to how we view the world. Both Longinus and Kant have lofty impressions of what it takes to create the sublime and thereby recognize and appreciate the sublime. Du Bois turns the conversation on its head, or to use Hubbard's term, he seeks to "reverse the deformation" that has occurred. Du Bois notes in *Souls of Black Folks* that there is a "longing to know" and discover the "mountain path to Canaan . . . leading to heights high enough to overlook life."[29] He continues,

> The journey at least gave leisure for reflection and self-examination; it changed the child of Emancipation to the youth with dawning self-consciousness, self-realization, self-respect. In those sombre forests of his striving his own soul rose before him, and he saw himself,—darkly as through a veil; and yet he saw in himself some faint revelation of his power, of his mission. He began to have a dim feeling that, to attain his place in the world, he must be himself, and not another. For the first time he sought to analyze the burden he bore upon his back, that dead-weight of social degradation partially masked behind a half-named Negro problem.[30]

Though the design of the dominant culture's positioning of the Negro is oppressive, demeaning, and amoral, the resolve within the Negro is to shift his or her focus toward Canaan or the land of promise to see and live into an alternative narrative that both counters and discredits the dominant narrative, resulting in progress. This progression opens the possibility of a type of universal access to the sublime.

So, what makes this a troubling philosophical juncture? "Troubling," here, is intended to be a positive thing in that the contextual locus for the discourse of sublimity makes room for many voices to enter the discussion. In this regard, the sublime ceases to be a set, stagnant, and sacred reality relegated for a select few. Rather, the sublime serves as a point of intersection of knowledge and power, at which, power "possesses" knowledge. This knowledge, whether experiential or academic, benefits the human being's engagement with the world to a certain point. There comes a time or space in which an expression is required that represents a coupling of knowledge with power. For the artist, this coupling results in a masterpiece that is critically acclaimed or disdained. When Hubbard argues for the invention of the sublime for blacks, his sight of engagement is narrow. It is clear Du Bois is not inventing the sublime; he is presenting an artistic expression of a pre-existing reality for black people. Moreover, Du Bois is living into a tradition within black art that has been established by Phillis Wheatley, for her engagement with the sublime troubles the normative philosophical point of departure. Hence, her use of the sublime clearly emerges from within her cultural experience or hermeneutic that can then be applied to aid others in visualizing this type of beauty.

It is as though the "heavenly muse" endows Phillis Wheatley with the artistic lens to see beauty in the embattled Word, the Messiah. The interplay among lines 5, 7, and 8 cannot be overlooked:

> Why thus enrob'd delights he to appear
> . . .
> Compress'd in wrath the swelling wine-press groan'd,
> It bled, and pour'd the gushing purple round.[31]

Wheatley is ironically referring to the Word as a winepress. Significantly, the winepress is a tool, a machine, a device that extracts essential elements from grapes in the production of wine. Assuming the type of winepress Wheatley is referring to is the basket press or some variation, the grapes must be crushed before they are poured into the basket to be pressed. Wheatley is not suggesting that the grapes are bleeding; they are already crushed. She does, however, intimate that the winepress is bleeding between the slats of the basket, "gushing purple round."[32] It is the process or act of taking in the crushed grapes that results in the swelling and subsequent bleeding. Yet, this is all a delight for the war-embattled Messiah. The ensuing statement from this "Almighty Savior" confirms his delight.

The poet locates the beauty within war by transforming the Savior's "martial glories" to "dazzling glories."[33] By using the winepress imagery to describe the sacrificial work of Christ, Wheatley gives voice to the savior of the world. In the biblical text, Isaiah does not give voice to the divine in the same manner. Isaiah suggests the Messiah had been treading the winepress alone (perceptively the winepress of God's wrath) by crushing the enemies of the children of God, enemies like Edom.[34] Wheatley's personifying of the winepress results in an opportunity for the reader to build upon the Messiah's textual treading to see and examine the Messiah as winepress. Ascribing the winepress's characteristics/properties to the Messiah enables Wheatley to change the nature of the Savior's articulation from one of reflection on a future redemption to one that is perpetually available now. The Messiah's statement is artistically presented as follows:

> "Mine was the act," th' Almighty Saviour said,
> And shook the dazzling glories of his head,
> "When all forsook I trod the press alone,
> And conquer'd by omnipotence my own;
> For man's release sustain'd the pond'rous load,
> For man the wrath of an immortal God:
> To execute th' Eternal's dread command
> My soul I sacrific'd with willing hand;
> Sinless I stood before the avenging frown,
> Atoning thus for vices not my own."[35]

The conversation mirrors the biblical account to a point. Lines 9 through 16 are fairly close to verses 3 through 6. Yet, there is a point of startling contention between the accounts. In lines 17 and 18, the Messiah suggests he stood sinless "before the avenging frown, / Atoning thus for vices not my own." The Messiah is reflecting upon an act to save someone else from what appears to be a cyclical sin-riddled reality. The use of the term "vices" lends one to assume the Messiah is combating a habitual moral failing or potentially rescuing those who are oppressed as a result of the very same moral failing.

In Isaiah's account, however, contention arises initially in verse 5. The prophet notes, "Mine own arm brought salvation unto me" (verse 5). This seeming self-serving rationale for fighting and retribution, though emblematic of many Old Testament presentations of a vengeful God, does not reflect the self-sacrificing redeemer of the New Testament. This is where the contention emerges between Isaiah's account and Wheatley's account. To redeem this passage in Isaiah, Wheatley seeks out the salvific work of Christ within the sixty-third chapter of Isaiah. It is important to note that most biblical textual analysis of Isaiah 63 tends to end with commentary on verse 6 and the vengeful redemptive narrative. However, Wheatley, by extending the vision into the setup of an extended prayer of lament, forces the committed scholar to ask the question of relation. Basically, Wheatley uses verses 7 and 8 as the basis for her engagement with the vengeful redemption of verses 1 through 6. For her, relationship trumps revenge. Verses 7 and 8 of Isaiah 63 have eternal import for Wheatley. She sets up her analysis of these verses and her understanding of refuge, resilience, and resistance in lines 19 through 23. Understanding the Messiah has performed these redemptive acts without assistance or "succours," Wheatley, as prophet, comments on her belief as to why this is the case, "His own omnipotence sustain'd the fight, / His vengeance sunk the haughty foes in night" (lines 21–22). Her stance as a homoousian is significant here.[36] The Messiah possesses the same power as YHWH and is therefore omnipotent. For that reason, there is no earthly or human power that can stand against the omnipotent savior.

Here, too, Wheatley introduces ever so subtly the reality of the morally bankrupt slavocracy. The object of the Messiah's vengeance is those who are considered haughty. Echoes of Matthew 23 emerge here as the evangelist writes,

> Then spake Jesus to the multitude, and to his disciples,
> Saying The scribes and the Pharisees sit in Moses' seat:
> All therefore whatsoever they bid you observe, that observe and do; but do not ye after their works: for they say, and do not.
> For they bind heavy burdens and grievous to be borne, and lay them on men's shoulders; but they themselves will not move them with one of their fingers.
> But all their works they do for to be seen of men: they make broad their phylacteries, and enlarge the borders of their garments,
> And love the uppermost rooms at feasts, and the chief seats in the synagogues,
> And greetings in the markets, and to be called of men, Rabbi, Rabbi.
> But be not ye called Rabbi: for one is your Master, even Christ; and all ye are brethren.
> And call no man your father upon the earth: for one is your Father, which is in heaven.
> Neither be ye called masters: for one is your Master, even Christ.
> But he that is greatest among you shall be your servant.
> And whosoever shall exalt himself shall be abased; and he that shall humble himself shall be exalted.[37]

Here, we encounter a major indictment that Jesus gives to those who desire to occupy certain spaces. When one looks at the occupant that Jesus is referring to, we first notice that Jesus says very simply that the Scribes and the Pharisees sit in Moses's seat. The Scribes and the Pharisees occupy Moses's seat. That means that the scribes and the Pharisees sit in a seat that does not necessarily belong to them. They have been grafted in by an act of divine grace and mercy. They are sitting in the seat of Moses. Jesus in essence asserts that the haughty, self-interest-protecting, and self-promoting persons enjoy the privilege of position while exploiting the privilege of power. The position that they hold is one that is, by its very nature, a Liberation position. It is a position that inherently goes against the grain of the established order, speaking truth to power, and wielding the support of Yahweh.

The Scribes and Pharisees were the ones that were called to help people comply with the law established on Mount Sinai by God through Moses. Notice, it is not the law of Moses, but it's the law established through Moses because the Ten Commandments were the ones that God gave to Moses to write down, meaning they came from God. The Scribes and Pharisees have just been in a conversation with the Lord. The Pharisees came to Jesus and said, "Master, which is the great commandment in the law?" Jesus said unto him, "Thou shalt love the Lord thy God with all thy heart, and with all thy soul, and with all thy mind. This is the first and great commandment. And the second is like unto it, Thou shalt love thy neighbour as thyself. On these two commandments hang all the law and the prophets."[38] In other words, everything that the Scribes and Pharisees stand for, everything that the Scribes and Pharisees protect, everything that the Scribes and Pharisees uphold, everything that the Scribes and Pharisees argue about hinges on these two laws: love the Lord your God with all your heart, mind, and soul. And love your neighbor as yourself. If you do these two things, then you automatically fulfill the ten commandments that came through Moses, and you automatically fulfill any and everything that the prophets of God have espoused about how God operates in the world. And so, the Scribes and Pharisees are in the position to uphold the law, and in the position to make the law, and in the position to enforce the law, yet they fail to consistently do so because they enjoy the privilege of position to exploit the privilege of power.

Jesus notes, "Do and observe whatever they tell you but not the works they do for they preach, but do not practice."[39] Wheatley witnesses those who occupy the position or the seat of Moses, the seat of the one who's supposed to be leading, guiding, and directing, and they occupy these positions, yet they do not follow through on the laws themselves. They are above the law. They can do any and everything that they desire without consequences because they are committed to the Slavocracy.

The occupant engorges in the privilege of popularity. Jesus says in verse 5, "All their works they do for to be seen of men."[40] He goes on to say, "[They] love the uppermost rooms at feasts, and the chief seats in the synagogues, [a]nd greetings in the markets, and to be called of men, Rabbi, Rabbi."[41] Jesus is saying the Scribes and Pharisees live by public opinion.

Wheatley, like Jesus, speaks for the divine promoter, hence she inserts her Christocentric lens into this prophetic narrative interpretation to point to a new reality within the Slavocracy. The text says very clearly, "Whosoever shall exalt himself shall be abased; and he that shall humble himself shall be exalted."[42] Frederick Douglass, Harriet Jacobs, and others who would follow echo Wheatley's and Jesus's sentiment of the haughty nature of white Americans, specifically noting the morally bankrupt nature of some of the most religious masters.

Wheatley's insistence on moral uprightness in the midst of the Slavocracy is significant. The contradictory nature of the American Christian's profession and practice serves as the foundation for Wheatley's concept of liberation. There is a system in place that Wheatley leads in seeking to upend to shed light on nature's or God's design for humanity.

There are clear consequences for not conforming to God's vision for humanity. These enemies progress lay dying and dead at the feet of the Messiah. The dying are particularly intriguing. It would seem Wheatley is suggesting any and all deniers of the equality of humanity are ultimately enemies of God. This proposition makes sense and relates to the integrity of the biblical account, for verses 7 and 8 point to what it means to be on God's side, in the house of Israel. Here, Wheatley pulls on the narrative presented in Isaiah 34 to expound further on the significance of the relationship between God and the House of Israel or Zion. Zion or the House of Israel represents God's covenantal people. God will avenge God's people and institute "the year of recompences for the controversy of Zion."[43] Wheatley's descriptor of Zion as "thy Zion" bespeaks an alternative possession to that of the Slavocracy. If the slaveholders are the enemies of the slave, then the slaveholders are also enemies of the slave's God. For, God is a God of the oppressed. Though these "foes may rage," as "cunning" and resourceful as they may be, they will ultimately fall.

In this moment, Wheatley returns to or solidifies her role as griot and prophet by converging Armah's notion of resilience and resistance, yet she adds the necessary notion or concept of refuge: "Yet she serenely on thy bosom lies, / Smiles at their arts, and all their force defies."[44] The enslaved African in America can find refuge on the "bosom" of the "Great God" who stands by his commitment to provide protection. Having the confidence of God's protection, the chattel can smile at the "arts" or conniving ways of the slavocracy exhibiting resilience despite the odds. It is through this commitment to resilience that the overall forces of evil are defied. Hence, the prophet Phillis Wheatley is suggesting to the slave, if you take refuge in God, you will gain resilience because of your closeness to God, and you will be able to be benefactors of resistance through God. For God said, "Surely they are my people, children that will not lie: so he was their Savior."[45] Wheatley is suggesting that the mind is the seat of identity politics. In essence, "I think; therefore, I am" reimagined to account for the experience of enslaved Africans in America.[46] If you believe or can conceive of a reality in which you are no longer a slave, you can begin to live into that new life, regardless of present position. The mind or individual consciousness, then, is the seat of redemptive creation.

NOTES

1. Wheatley, "Isaiah lxiii.1–8," in *Poems on Various Subjects*, pp. 60–61, lines 1–30.
2. Is. 63:1–8 (KJV).
3. The griots emerge out of West Africa as wordsmiths who are keepers of the tradition and advisors to the royal families. According to the Mande, most likely a familiar tribe to Wheatley, they are called jali (jalimuso for women). Importantly, the jaliyaa (the craft of the jail) is passed down through generations from mother to daughter and father to son. See E. L. Cyrs, "The Ancient Craft of Jaliyaa," in *Baba the Storyteller*.
4. Armah, *The Eloquence of the Scribes*, 12.
5. Armah, 116.
6. Armah, 117–18.
7. Armah further explains, "An iconic representation of the griots' insight—that with the triumph of the Europeans Africa entered a time of loss, and that we have important memory work to do if we are to recover what we lost—is the image of the Sankofa bird. The bird is shown in mid-flight: history flows on. Its forward motion is not in doubt; nevertheless, the bird is aware of having dropped something valuable, indeed, indispensable. It therefore casts its vision backward, not with any intention of reversing time and returning to the past to live there, but with the purpose of retrieving from past time just that element of value that should not have been lost, prior to continuing its interrupted motion" (118).
8. Wheatley, "Isaiah lxiii.1–8," pp. 60–61 (my emphasis).
9. Jn 1:1 (KJV).
10. Jn 1:14 (KJV).
11. Prothero, *American Jesus*, 9.
12. Prothero, 9.
13. Sanders, *Historical Figure of Jesus*, 1.
14. Guthrie, *The Word of the Lord*, 119.
15. Guthrie, 119.
16. Wheatley, "Isaiah lxiii.1–8," p. 60, lines 1–2.
17. Wheatley, "Isaiah lxiii.1–8," p. 60, lines 5–6.
18. Hubbard, "W.E.B. Du Bois and the Invention of the Sublime," 298.
19. Jefferson, *Notes on the State of Virginia*, 234.
20. I use the term *reasoned art* to illumine the paradox of the Eurocentric engagement with art, poetry, philosophy, and the like. Hubbard notes there was a definite need to define the sublime or give valuation to beauty: "The sublime is the gossamer thread of the imagination. It functions as a metasymbolic narrative that informs a people's relation to the Divine" (305). The sublime then determines the efficacy of one's soul.
21. Cahill and Larkin, "Aesthetics, Feeling, and Form," 243.
22. Cahill and Larkin, 243.

23. Otto, *The Idea of the Holy*, 12.
24. Hubbard, 299.
25. Roberts, *Awakening Verse*, 24.
26. Bernard, introduction to *Kant's Critique of Judgement*, by Immanuel Kant, xxi.
27. Bernard, xxi.
28. Bernard, xxii.
29. Du Bois, *The Souls of Black Folk*, 11.
30. Du Bois, 12.
31. Wheatley, "Isaiah lxiii. 1–8," p. 60, lines 5, 7–8.
32. Wheatley, "Isaiah lxiii. 1–8," p. 60, line 8.
33. Wheatley, "Isaiah lxiii. 1–8," p. 60, line 3, 10.
34. Hanson, *Isaiah 40–66*, 233–34.
35. Wheatley, "Isaiah lxiii. 1–8," pp. 60–61, lines 9–18.
36. *Homoousias* is the Council of Nicaea's theological understanding and conclusion that God and God's Son, though distinct, are of the same essence or substance.
37. Matt. 23:1–12 (KJV).
38. Matt. 22:36–40 (KJV).
39. Matt. 23:3 (KJV).
40. Matt. 23:5 (KJV).
41. Matt. 23:6–7 (KJV).
42. Matt. 23:12 (KJV).
43. Is. 34:8 (KJV).
44. Wheatley, "Isaiah lxiii. 1–8," p. 61, lines 29–30.
45. Is. 63:8 (KJV).
46. English translation of René Descartes's, *Cogito, ergo sum*.

Chapter 4

Created in the Imagination

On Imagination

THY various works, imperial queen, we see,
How bright their forms! how deck'd with pomp by thee!
Thy wond'rous acts in beauteous order stand,
And all attest how potent is thine hand.

From Helicon's refulgent heights attend,   5
Ye sacred choir, and my attempts befriend:
To tell her glories with a faithful tongue,
Ye blooming graces, triumph in my song.

Now here, now there, the roving Fancy flies,
Till some lov'd object strikes her wand'ring eyes,   10
Whose silken fetters all the senses bind,
And soft captivity involves the mind.

Imagination! who can sing thy force?
Or who describe the swiftness of thy course?
Soaring through air to find the bright abode,   15
Th' empyreal palace of the thund'ring God,
We on thy pinions can surpass the wind,
And leave the rolling universe behind:
From star to star the mental optics rove,
Measure the skies, and range the realms above.   20
There in one view we grasp the mighty whole,
Or with new worlds amaze th' unbounded soul.

Though Winter frowns to Fancy's raptur'd eyes
The fields may flourish, and gay scenes arise;
The frozen deeps may break their iron bands,   25
And bid their waters murmur o'er the sands.
Fair Flora may resume her fragrant reign,
And with her flow'ry riches deck the plain;
Sylvanus may diffuse his honours round,
And all the forest may with leaves be crown'd: 30

Show'rs may descend, and dews their gems disclose,
And nectar sparkle on the blooming rose.

Such is thy pow'r, nor are thine orders vain,
O thou the leader of the mental train:
In full perfection all thy works are wrought,   35
And thine the sceptre o'er the realms of thought.
Before thy throne the subject-passions bow,
Of subject-passions sov'reign ruler Thou;
At thy command joy rushes on the heart,
And through the glowing veins the spirits dart.   40

Fancy might now her silken pinions try
To rise from earth, and sweep th' expanse on high;
From Tithon's bed now might Aurora rise,
Her cheeks all glowing with celestial dies,
While a pure stream of light o'erflows the skies.   45
The monarch of the day I might behold,
And all the mountains tipt with radiant gold,
But I reluctant leave the pleasing views,
Which Fancy dresses to delight the Muse;
Winter austere forbids me to aspire,   50
And northern tempests damp the rising fire;
They chill the tides of Fancy's flowing sea,
Cease then, my song, cease the unequal lay.[1]

An Hymn to Humanity

To S. P. G. Esq;

I.
LO! for this dark terrestrial ball
Forsakes his azure-paved hall
  A prince of heav'nly birth!
Divine Humanity behold.
What wonders rise, what charms unfold   5
  At his descent to earth!

II.
The bosoms of the great and good
With wonder and delight he view'd,

And fix'd his empire there:
Him, close compressing to his breast,   10
The sire of gods and men address'd,
  "My son, my heav'nly fair!

III.
"Descend to earth, there place thy throne;
To succour man's afflicted son
  Each human heart inspire: 15
To act in bounties unconfin'd
Enlarge the close contracted mind,
  And fill it with thy fire."

IV.
Quick as the word, with swift career
He wings his course from star to star,   20
  And leaves the bright abode.
The Virtue did his charms impart;
Their G———y! then thy raptur'd heart
  Perceiv'd the rushing God:

V.
For when thy pitying eye did see   25
The languid muse in low degree,
  Then, then at thy desire
Descended the celestial nine;
O'er me methought they deign'd to shine,
  And deign'd to string my lyre.   30

VI.
Can Afric's muse forgetful prove?
Or can such friendship fail to move
  A tender human heart?
Immortal Friendship laurel-crown'd
The smiling Graces all surround   35
  With ev'ry heav'nly Art.[2]

"Let this mind be in you that was also in Christ Jesus."

—Philippians 2:5

THE CREATIVE ACT

The United Negro College Fund annually grants scholarships to numerous minority college students who would otherwise perhaps not have the opportunity to get a college education. The slogan or motto of the UNCF is "A mind is a terrible thing to waste." This statement, though coming some centuries later, echoes Wheatley's consciousness. As her master John Wheatley suggests, it is her own inner drive that compels her to learn all she can, and for what? Precisely, to prove that her mind is not an inconsequential commodity to be dismissed, ignored, or discarded. She uses her mind to reimagine a world that represents the original created order of things, thereby articulating agency for herself and a new reality for her people.

Creation in "On Imagination" is reflexive. For Wheatley, it is not merely reflective, for then her mission and aim would be more akin to James Weldon Johnson's in his poem "The Creation."[3] Rather, she pushes the envelope to take the reader on a journey to reflect on the past creative act in order to utilize the essence of that act to re-create a new present reality for America. By creation being reflexive, Wheatley is able to reimagine her reality in poetic form. In "On Imagination," she seeks to recast the process of creation. The need for this re-creation is evidenced by how far this supposed Christian nation had sojourned from a state of ordered chaos. Perhaps Wheatley, realizing God had already made an attempt at re-creation through the salvific offering of God's son, chooses to use her prophetic voice to unpack the imprint of Christ. The imprint of Christ can be summed up in the lyrical expression of Paul who suggests to the Philippian citizens,

> If there be therefore any consolation in Christ, if any comfort of love, if any fellowship of the Spirit, if any bowels and mercies, Fulfil ye my joy, that ye be likeminded, having the same love, being of one accord, of one mind. Let nothing be done through strife or vainglory; but in lowliness of mind let each esteem other better than themselves.
>
> Look not every man on his own things, but every man also on the things of others.
>
> Let this mind be in you, which was also in Christ Jesus: Who, being in the form of God, thought it not robbery to be equal with God: But made himself of no reputation, and took upon him the form of a servant, and was made in the likeness of men: And being found in fashion as a man, he humbled himself, and became obedient unto death, even the death of the cross. Wherefore God also hath highly exalted him, and given him a name which is above every name: That at the name of Jesus every knee should bow, of things in heaven, and things in earth, and things under the earth; And that every tongue should confess that Jesus Christ is Lord, to the glory of God the Father.[4]

The imprint of Christ in this passage is that of a sacrificial servant. Christ makes the choice to be "of no reputation" in order to adequately and efficiently serve humanity with humility. Based upon the passage, there is no objective or expectation of accolades or reward other than that of being recognized as "obedient unto death." The concept or theme of being obedient unto death is a common one within the African American preaching tradition, often expressed to eulogize individuals who live a life of service. The stark differentiation between "unto" and "until" serves as a significant distinction for one's rationale or motivation for service. The argument is that if the word "until" represents the culmination of something at a distinct endpoint, "unto," though an archaic form of "until," serves as a directional preposition that leaves room for a continuation or delivery of a thing. If the individual is serving unto death, it means that he or she is serving toward that end, which is actually a continuation of life as opposed to a culmination of life. The context is derived from this passage, noting that through death God will highly exalt those who choose to be sacrificial servants. The imprint, then, is the external exaltation that comes to bare out of divine (as opposed to selfish) design. So, if Christ's approach and mentality is the goal, it is incumbent upon the committed follower to use the same tools, particularly that of the mind, to make the choice to live a life of mutual sacrificial service and to look at every one as God does. Re-creation, then, is about reestablishing equality, and liberation is the primary requirement.

In "On Imagination," Wheatley continues her exploration of the doctrine of creation and focuses on the imagination in general but more particularly on the artist's ability to create a world that frees or liberates itself from the restrictions of the current world. The artist and imagination become a unified voice. Personifying Imagination or attributing specific godlike traits to Imagination, she employs creation imagery as she describes God's palace in the sky, air, thunder, wind, and a rolling universe:

> *Imagination!* Who can sing thy force?
> Or who describe the swiftness of thy course?
> Soaring through air to find the bright abode,
> Th' empyreal palace of the thund'ring God,
> We on thy pinions can surpass the wind,
> And leave the rolling universe behind:
> From star to star the mental optics rove,
> Measure the skies, and range the realms above.
> There in one view we grasp the mighty whole,
> Or with new worlds amaze th' unbounded soul.[5]

In lines 13–16, Imagination searches for a celestial palace on which to land. Art in the form of poetry, for Wheatley, serves as a conduit for the liberation of the mind, body, and soul. The liberation, in this instance, is not due to some form of rescue or salvation; liberation emerges or is created through Imagination. The personified Imagination is similar to the Word in the biblical account of the creation, for the Word is the conduit through which all things are created. According to the gospel account, "In the beginning was the Word, and the Word was with God, and the Word was God. . . . All things were made by him; and without him was not any thing made that was made."[6] Just as the Word (most commonly associated in Judeo-Christian circles with Jesus) is indispensable to the biblical account of creation, Imagination is indispensable to Wheatley's account of creation. Imagination swiftly seeks out and establishes the space for the creation of the new world. According to the poem, the process of creation through Imagination is indescribable, and the act of creation is comparable only to the thunderous power of God.[7] Wheatley establishes Imagination as the ultimate force of creation.

Creation for Wheatley is comparable to the creation in the Bible. First, both processes involve the imagination, being able to create something out of nothing. As Wheatley's personified Imagination commences the creative process, she juxtaposes this poetic creative act with that of the biblical creation to note the uniqueness of the quality. Second, Wheatley's Imagination imposes her will on a waiting canvas, creating with "force" and "swiftness." Finally, Wheatley gives her Imagination a divine quality by referring to it as "Soaring through the air to find the bright abode, / Th' empyreal palace of the thund'ring God."[8] Hence, the artist as creator is godlike, for in the beginning, God created humankind "in [God's] image, after [God's] likeness."[9]

Wheatley continues this theme of creation in lines 17–22 noting that Imagination, through its creative power, is the impetus for the liberation of humanity. Only with Imagination can one, as a part of God's creation, surpass the wind and the universe. It is as though Imagination possesses the artist as the artist possess Imagination. It is this dual possession that perfects the created world. God, as divine artist, creates through Imagination. As noted in the earlier Gospel of John account of creation, Imagination is not just with God but actually is God. In this way, Imagination almost becomes one with creation as the mind's eye scans the stars and measures the skies. Through Imagination, the artist sees beyond the confines of his or her reality and pulls into view a constructed world that is free. At this point in the poem, lines of distinction between God, Imagination, and creation become blurred. The lines conclude with a testament of the oneness of Imagination and creation—"There in one view we grasp the mighty whole."[10] Due to the fluidity in the relationship among God, Imagination, and creation, that which is "imagined" can become reality. The imagined new world is to emerge seemingly against the odds resulting in a space of amazing peace and freedom. Significantly, in this imagined new world, the soul is unbound, free to strive and create.

Just as the lines of demarcation among God, Imagination, and creation are blurred, Wheatley also successfully blurs the lines of demarcation between black people and white people, rich and poor through her subversive use of language and imagery. Novelist Richard Wright commented on Wheatley's use of imagination in 1945 noting, "Whatever its qualities as poetry, ["On Imagination"] records the feelings of a Negro reacting not as a Negro, but as a human being."[11] Wright suggests that Wheatley has produced a poem that transcends race and culture to highlight the equality of humanity. Still, critics like James Weldon Johnson, Vernon Loggins, Benjamin Brawley, Sterling A. Brown, and Arthur P. Davis note Wheatley's objective view as detrimental to the cause of liberation. Davis even reads Wright's favorable commentary as one noting Wheatley's ownership of her humanity at the expense of her blackness: "She was refreshingly and fortunately 'detached,' and as a consequence, she was free to write 'not as a Negro, but as a human being.'"[12] By detached, Davis is referring to Wheatley's status as a free black who is writing about an enslaved and oppressed black people's plight. Though Davis argues that Wheatley's point of departure in "On Imagination" is "detached," it is necessary to understand that it is actually her attachment to the black community, slavery, and the injustices experienced by her people that enables her to write with Imagination in a "detached" way. She creates an alternative reality from within, and, in so doing, exhibits the true "unbounded soul" of black America, thereby making her appeal palatable to the white readership.

More contemporary scholarship on the poem situates Wheatley as the central object of the poem. For instance, Hilene Flanzbaum notes that the poem "begins with the standard abdication: Wheatley professes impotence before the divine compulsion," ultimately resulting in Wheatley's imagery transforming "slavery into freedom."[13] Imagination in this instance becomes Wheatley's imagination, since we possess creative capacity, and when "the flight of imagination is over; she can defeat neither nature nor bondage, and Wheatley—nothing if not a realist—acknowledges that her ascent into the heavens has been only temporary."[14] Flanzbaum suggests that "On Imagination" serves as an articulation of Wheatley's momentary intoxication with freedom and subsequent return to reality. This reading, plausible as it may be, proves flawed. Placing Wheatley at the center of the poem ignores her affinity with the enslaved. Her deference to "divine compulsion," the creation of a new world, and the transformation of slavery into freedom is implemented not as an escapist ploy but, rather, as reverence, appreciation, and allegiance to the power of divine creation, a divinity that created all humans as equals. In her articulation of divine creation as essential for humanity, Wheatley pushes the reader to consider freedom as a right accessible to all;

and this articulation of creation reveals the ways her theology is undergird by liberation for the enslaved.

THE COMMITTED RESPONSE

It is through this understanding of creation as an imaginative act that Wheatley sets up her plea for re-creation. Re-creation serves as the committed and proper response to God's creative act. If the imagination is the seat of creation, then humanity writ large serves as the seat of re-creation, for they are the ones who are operating as the ambassadors of God. Through "Hymn to Humanity" Wheatley argues for a need to re-create what has been created. She furthers her engagement with the concept of re-creation and the redemptive work of Christ through this poem. It would seem this poem diverts from Wheatley's traditional engagement with humanity, for in many of her poems, she critiques humanity, often with lyrical indictments. However, in this poem she has a much more nuanced approach. As a student of mythologies and mystical faith traditions, her awareness of the need for re-creation does not emerge from her mind nor the feeble mind of mortals. Rather, she artistically recounts God's desire to re-create that which God has already created. It is more than a revision, for a revision would mean that the current foundation is stable enough to simply adjust certain aspects of humanity to present an acceptable reality. Every educator knows there is a difference between student-submitted essays that are able to be revised versus those essays that need to be re-composed. The initial idea may have worked and sounded great, but somewhere along the way, the details and supporting ideas became skewed and detached from that original idea. Such is the case with humanity in God's eyes per Wheatley, so there is a need to re-create through radical redemption.

Wheatley's initial engagement with re-creation or God's redemptive work through "Hymn to Humanity" is found within her title of the poem. Since a hymn is traditionally viewed as a song or poem of praise to God, it is important to note that Wheatley's use of the term and its placement suggests an alternate construction. This hymn is a hymn to humanity, not divinity. The question for the committed scholar becomes, why does Wheatley misuse the word "HYMN?" Perhaps, Wheatley is using "HYMN" as a homonym. "HYMN" is in all capital letters, and "Humanity" is not in the early print versions.[15] Elizabeth J. West, engaging John S. Mbiti, notes that the "significance of the sun in Wheatley's spiritual cosmos is evident in her corresponding poetic contemplations on nature,"[16] particularly in "An HYMN to the Morning" and "An HYMN to the Evening."[17] The sun is considered the "king of day" and "him who gives light, / And draws the sable curtains of the night."[18] The sun, then is not only the king of the day and the one who gives light but also the one who permits night to emerge. The "he" Wheatley is referring to is the sun, which is clearly a nod to African cosmology; however, it is also consistent, based on her use of the sun, with the Judeo-Christian understanding of the Son as one with God who has the authority over both the day and night. Similarly, in "An HYMN to Humanity," I suggest there are at least two things happening. First, Wheatley is suggesting that the hymn is more significant in some way than humanity. Second, Wheatley is pointing to a homonym for "Hymn," namely "Him." With this reasoning, the HYMN to Humanity is actually the HIM to Humanity. This "Him," when in printed literature (and throughout much of Wheatley's poetry), often coincides with God or Jesus. If this is Wheatley's appropriation of the term, the decision to differentiate between the capitalization of HYMN and Humanity is purposeful, for both God and God through Jesus are uniquely distinct from humanity. If Jesus is the Hymn, then Jesus is seeking a way to honor or praise humanity. This, I contend, is the mission Wheatley embarks on through this poem. She is seeking to articulate the desire of God through Christ to sing to humanity:

> LO! for this dark terrestrial ball
> Forsakes his azure-paved hall
> A prince of heav'nly birth!
> Divine Humanity behold.
> What wonders rise, what charms unfold
> At his descent to earth![19]

Wheatley's description of the earth as a "dark terrestrial ball" is most likely a suggestion of the sinful nature of humanity. This current reality apparently stands in opposition to the divine intent, for the poet continues that the earth has forsaken "his azure paved hall." Creation has determined the sky to be "azure" or cloudless; however, this is apparently not the case since the poet is making an announcement about a wondrous arrival. Wheatley, much like the angel Gabriel, has been sent with this urgent announcement that a "prince of heav'nly birth" will arrive as a baby for the benefit of creation. He is, however, descending from heaven to earth, meaning he is not simply human but both human and divine, Charles Wesley's incarnate deity. Interestingly, Wheatley also attempts to encourage humanity to prepare for the arrival, noting that they too have divine qualities; she tells them (Divine *Humanity*) to behold this prince who will come with mighty power and wonders. Her celebratory tenor mirrors that of Charles Wesley's 1739 hymn, which was adapted by George Whitefield in 1754 entitled "Hark! The Herald Angels Sing"

> Hark! The herald angels sing,
> "Glory to the newborn King!

> Peace on earth and mercy mild,
> God and sinners reconciled."
> Joyful, all ye nations rise,
> Join the triumph of the skies,
> With th'angelic host proclaim:
> "Christ is born in Bethlehem."
> Hark! The herald angels sing,
> "Glory to the newborn King!"
>
> Christ by highest heav'n adored,
> Christ the everlasting Lord!
> Late in time behold Him come,
> Offspring of a Virgin's womb.
> Veiled in flesh the Godhead see,
> Hail the incarnate Deity,
> Pleased as man with man to dwell,
> Jesus, our Emmanuel.
> Hark! The herald angels sing,
> "Glory to the newborn King!"
>
> Hail the heav'n-born Prince of Peace!
> Hail the Son of Righteousness!
> Light and life to all He brings,
> Ris'n with healing in His wings.
> Mild He lays His glory by,
> Born that man no more may die,
> Born to raise the sons of earth,
> Born to give them second birth.
> Hark! The herald angels sing,
> "Glory to the newborn King!"[20]

Wheatley would have undoubtedly been keenly aware of this hymn given her familiarity with Whitefield and the Wesleys, Charles and John, all of whom are founding members of Methodism. This is significant because, she would have been familiar with the earlier versions of both 1739 and 1758, which read differently from the lines above. Granted the above lines do appear in the earlier versions; however, there are lines omitted from the version that often appears in standard hymnals. The original seventh through tenth verses that Wheatley would have been familiar with read as follows:

> Come, Desire of Nations, come,
> Fix in Us thy humble Home,

> Rise, the Woman's Conqu'ring Seed,
> Bruise in Us the Serpent's Head.
> Now display thy saving Pow'r,
> Ruin'd Nature now restore,
> Now in Mystic Union join
> Thine to Ours, and Ours to Thine.
> Adam's Likeness, Lord, efface,
> Stamp thy Image in its Place,
> Second Adam from above,
> Reinstate us in thy Love.
> Let us Thee, tho' lost, regain,
> Thee, the Life, the Inner Man:
> O! to All Thyself impart,
> Form'd in each Believing Heart.[21]

Wheatley seems to focus her thrust on these concluding lines of the hymn, for she is insistent on the holiness of God, required humility of humanity, the redemptive opportunity presented to "Ruin'd Nature" (Wesley), and the reinstatement or restoration that can mystically occur to brighten this "dark terrestrial ball."[22] Moreover, the work of redemption is both collective and individual.

Wheatley personalizes the redemptive work of Christ. She notes,

> For when thy pitying eye did see
> The languid muse in low degree,
>   Then, then at thy desire
> Descended the celestial nine;
> O'er me methought they deign'd to shine,
>   And deign'd to string my lyre.[23]

She suggests that the "prince of heav'nly birth" has seen her and pitied or had compassion for her "low degree."[24] The reason for her current status is her inability to create. She seemingly refers to herself as the "languid muse." In most instances, Wheatley invokes the "muses" in the plural form. Here, however, she uses the singular. In this instance, the reader is led to understand her as not referring to the nine goddesses of the arts, largely because they are invoked two lines later. It is safe to assume she is referring to the artist's internal inspiration. She is at best uninspired, languid. Given her state, one would think she would cry out for help or an alternative source of inspiration. Such is not the case; rather, she notes that at "thy desire" help descended. At whose desire? Suggestively, at the desire of the Lord who has been watching her and has seen her current state. This is central to Wheatley's soteriological argument, for part of the distinctiveness of Judeo-Christian theology is the gracious sacrifice of the Son of God. Jesus chooses to die for humanity though they have done nothing necessarily to deserve that redemptive act. It is at his own desire. The help comes in the presence of the celestial nine. Here again, Wheatley conflates the Christian narrative with that of the Roman and Greek mythologies as if to say that even the pagan gods and goddesses of antiquity are subject and beholden to the Creator and Savior. These angelic beings come to assist the artist in her low degree. They deign or condescend to her level to aid her. It is much like the stories within varying Gospel accounts of Jesus condescending to the level of people who are hurting or struggling to help them. Wheatley then gives us the rationale for her current state. Her lyre needs to be restrung. Stringed instruments are unable to function without strings. Music cannot be made without strings, hence the artist cannot perform or worship properly. The divine nine restring her lyre enabling her then to choose to either try to play the song again or remain in her current state with a functioning lyre. Wheatley issues this challenge to her readers in hopes that they will choose the former because of this underserved opportunity. Wheatley's testimony helps to accent and clarify the process of redemption for her readers, for it comes on the heels of her presentation of what redemption through re-creation looks like.

As mentioned in the opening of the poem and in her testimonial, Christ leaves heaven and chooses to aid Wheatley. As John writes in Revelation 21, there is a certain condition being met through the poet's words. That condition is the human condition of the misuse of grace. Fallen humanity has failed to adequately appreciate creation, hence God is forced to make a choice of either destruction or salvation. When the flood waters came and wiped out all of Noah's contemporaries, God was utilizing a physical corrective for fallen humanity (a point I will return to). In this instance, through Christ, God is using a spiritual corrective, a holy fire of sorts. Wheatley's nod to the interventional Christ is almost apocalyptic in the insertion of the language of descent, which mirrors that of the author of Revelation: "And I heard a great voice out of heaven saying, Behold, the tabernacle of God is with men, and he will dwell with them, and they shall be his people, and God himself shall be with them, and be their God."[25] The voice out of heaven that utters this decree is presumably the Spirit of God since later John situates commentary as belonging to the one sitting on the throne. Wheatley's infatuation with the plight of humanity and the grace of God is tied to her description and intent of the re-creative act. She defines re-creation through five actions: descent, support, inspiration, enlargement, and infusion.

> The bosoms of the great and good
> With wonder and delight he view'd,
> And fix'd his empire there:

> Him, close compressing to his breast,
> The sire of gods and men address'd,
> "My son, my heav'nly fair!
> "Descend to earth, there place thy throne;
> To succour man's afflicted son
> Each human heart inspire:
> To act in bounties unconfin'd
> Enlarge the close contracted mind,
> And fill it with thy fire."[26]

The concept of descending is significant for Wheatley for she invokes it here in line 13, previously in line 6, and later in her moment of personal testimony. This act of descent is the first step in Re-creation. God must "descend to earth" for the sake of inhabitance. The reader is sure of God's desire to inhabit because he expresses to God's son to place his throne in earth. This descent and placement, however, is but the physical manifestation of the commencement of an inspirational or internal process, for Wheatley reports that "[t]he bosoms of the great and good / With wonder and delight he view'd, / And fix'd his empire there."[27] The work of descent begins with an impression upon the "bosoms" or hearts of some "great and good" people who appropriately revere God. Hence, there will be some who will accept the physical imposition of his throne because they have already made space for his lordship within their hearts. Conversely, there will be those who do not readily receive the inhabitance of the Lord.

Regardless of the resistance by some, the reason for his descent is "to succour man's afflicted son."[28] At the outset, this statement seems a bit misplaced. My interpretation, however, is based on the identity of "man's afflicted son." On the one hand, Wheatley could be referring to humanity in general. On the other hand, she could be implicating an afflicted or fallen segment of humanity. Significantly, based on the context of the poem, the latter is most certainly the case. However, there are multiple possible and appropriate interpretations within that framework. It can be inferred that man's afflicted son represents the descendants of a powerful and influential people—for example, Europeans writ large. The afflicted sons in this instance are white Americans, afflicted internally because of their inability to appreciate diversity within humanity. However, using an Africentric interpretive lens considering the context of Wheatley's body of work, man's afflicted son can refer to the darker peoples of America and their struggle. That word "afflicted" can be understood as an internal disposition, as in the aforementioned inference, or as an external agent or course of events that result in one's affliction. As the Psalmist has noted, "It is good for me that I have been afflicted; that I might learn thy statutes."[29] The external affliction leaves the subject in a seemingly helpless state; yet, the design is clear to the "great and good" segment of humanity who, though afflicted, know the benefit of submission to help or support from above. The design is for the sake of advancement. As the psalmist classifies it, it is a participatory learning opportunity that results in a deeper knowledge of and commitment to the will of God. The "succour" or help descends despite or perhaps because of the negro's affliction.

The third action is to inspire each human heart. There is not much inspiration that is needed for the "great and good" people who are already accepting of the throne of God, so the focus is on the remaining demographic. Wheatley suggests, by implication, there is a need to inspire the slaveholding individuals in the South and the unsympathetic whites and apathetic negroes in the North to fight for the cause of liberation of those who are insensibly afflicted. In other words, there is a need to inspire potential co-creators and collaborators in this divine re-creation process.

This inspiration fuels the fourth action, which is to "[e]nlarge the close contracted mind."[30] The only way one can operate or "act in bounties unconfin'd" is to have an expansion of the mind.[31] The same mind, in other words, that was in this creative Christ must be adopted by humanity: *Cogito ergo sum*. This statement attributed to René Descartes is translated into English as "I think, therefore I am." It is notable that Wheatley uses the spirit of this mantra, potentially inspired by the words of the Apostle Paul in Philippians 2, as a part of the re-creative process. For slave and free alike, it is impossible to live into a new reality without inspiration to act and the subsequent enlargement of your conceptualization of the self and the world. The process of enlargement makes room for dreaming and hoping, which are necessary for re-creation.

The fifth and final action that is taken in this process of re-creation is an infusion. Wheatley records "fill it with thy fire."[32] Here, she concludes the instructions from God to the Son of God with a command to not just inspire but to fill or infuse. That the element of use is fire is significant. Fire has both refining and purifying properties. When used improperly, fire can simply destroy, but, in the right hands, fire can create beauty. The fire suggested in this command has both salvific and re-creative implications. As noted earlier, when the children of God were disobedient and the world seemed dark in the Genesis account of scripture, God sent rain and flood waters to destroy the earth. During this time, he spared Noah and his family, along with the animals. When Noah finally emerges from the security of the ark, he steps out into a "new world" that had been purified by the waters. The promise God makes with Noah and his descendants is that he would not destroy the world with water again; rather, he would use fire. This fire Wheatley suggests is not meant to destroy the land and, subsequently, purify it. This fire is meant to purify the heart. The fire works to refine the heart of man to prompt him to partner with this "prince of heav'nly birth" to re-create a sin sick nation.[33]

Wheatley justifies the five actions of re-creation by expounding on the purpose of Jesus's mission. In the fourth stanza, Wheatley states that Christ's mission is to impart virtue. The irony of Wheatley's diction is that it causes the reader to assume virtue is a foreign concept or reality for humanity. Otherwise, she would have stated that Christ came to restore virtue. Restoration is not the goal. The common understanding of virtue works to drive Wheatley's argument forward; however, one cannot overlook her choice to italicize and capitalize "*Virtue.*" Traditionally, virtue would refer to a good thing or some sort of moral quality; however, in this case, it seems Wheatley is attempting to reach beyond the classic understandings of virtue to present a uniquely Africentric concept of virtue, which predates any Latin constructions of virtue. Wheatley reports, "The *Virtue* did his charms impart."[34] Not *a* virtue, nor *many* virtues; rather, *the* Virtue is imparted.[35] The ultimacy virtue as a concept or trait is clearly suggested here. This conceptualization points even beyond the Judeo-Christian hierarchy of angelic beings, for there is one, singular Virtue. Christ is said to impart Virtue through charms. More than likely these charms represent the sayings of Christ that traditionally are recognized as having a mystical or magical quality. Based on Wheatley's prior assertions in this poem, the Virtue could manifest as the cumulative, transformative, love-centric expression of Christ's sayings about the equality of humanity. If so, Wheatley is naming the goddess Maât as Virtue. Ayi Kwei Armah states, "There are cosmic laws regulating reality at all levels. . . . The presiding rule is balance, justice."[36] This concept of balance and justice is "symbolized by the female deity Maât."[37] Maât serves as the ultimate moral force in the universe, compelling individuals to treat others with dignity and respect. There is an imbalance within Wheatley's America. There is racial imbalance, gender imbalance, socioeconomic imbalance, legislative imbalance, and spiritual imbalance as a result of false notions of divine right and American exceptionalism. Justice must emerge in order to reclaim balance and, thereby, impart Virtue. Yet, the challenge lay in the system itself, for domination politics and unbridled raced "power is not about balance and justice."[38]

The charms or sayings of Christ work to demolish the temples of imbalance and injustice erected by a slaveholding, humanity-denying culture. Wheatley observes the significance of these sayings, noting "[t]heir glory," for these words are words of both affirmation and relocation. Christ simultaneously affirms personhood while relocating the slave's body politic. It is not until Christ imparts Virtue that humanity's eyes are opened to the import of God's plan. Wheatley signifies this revelation with the conditional transition "then."[39] It is after the glory of Christ's charms emerge to impart Virtue that the human heart is exalted or elevated to the realm of the divine. Here, the object of God's preoccupation gains a new perspective and orientation. Wheatley even notes that the "raptur'd" or enlightened individual catches a perceptive glimpse of the "rushing God" who desires for a swift redirection. God's desire is that the urgency displayed in the celestial realm will be matched by all creation.

At the intersection of hope and fear, Wheatley stands as poet-theologian to utter a prophetic message in the tradition of the American Jeremiad with the cosmic picture of unity, friendship, and inspiration as the substance of the re-created reality. Sacvan Bercovitch proffers, the American Jeremiad "posits a movement from promise to experience—from the ideal of community to the shortcomings of community life—and thence forward, with prophetic assurance, toward the resolution that incorporates (as it transforms) both the promise and the condemnation."[40] Though some scholars suggest the American Jeremiad only addresses individual sin and communal sin with no regard for institutional sin and subsequent reform, a theocentric approach to understanding the American Jeremiad reveals the social relevance of individual responsibility to transform institutions. Wheatley capitalizes on the concept of communal social responsibility. If you can change or transform the way an individual sees and performs in the world, that individual will seek to change every institution with which she or he is affiliated. We find in the final stanza Wheatley's prophetic revelation of re-creation:

> Can *Afric's* muse forgetful prove?
> Or can such friendship fail to move
> A tender human heart?
> Immortal *Friendship* laurel-crown'd
> The smiling *Graces* all surround
> With ev'ry heav'nly *Art*.[41]

Upon Christ's filling the hearts of humanity, the kingdom is realized, for the seat of the kingdom is now the human heart. This bond or friendship is unlike any other due to the power dwelling in Christ. When the heart is wed to the divine, the outcome is always new and transcendent. The "Immortal *Friendship*" allows for acclaim and praise to abound. In this way, humanity is exalted. However, this exaltation is not for self-aggrandizement purposes; Wheatley suggests that as Christ is exalted genuinely by the human heart, humanity enters an eternally mutually beneficial redemptive partnership or co-creation—in this case, re-creation—that manifests in the form of art. This re-creation can also be classified as salvation.

NOTES

1. Wheatley, "On Imagination," in *Poems on Various Subjects*, pp. 65–68, lines 1–53.
2. Wheatley, "An Hymn to Humanity," in *Poems on Various Subjects*, pp. 95–97, lines 1–36.
3. Johnson crafts an artistic rendering of the Creation story found in Genesis. His account is meant to invited readers into the world of Genesis and reflect upon the beauty of creation, inclusive of God's final creative act—humankind.
4. Phil. 2:1–11 (KJV).
5. Wheatley, "On Imagination," p. 66, lines 13–22.
6. Jn 1:1,3 (KJV).
7. Wheatley, "On Imagination," p. 66, line 16.
8. Wheatley, "On Imagination," p. 66, lines 15–16.
9. Gen. 1:26 (KJV).
10. Wheatley, "On Imagination," p. 66, line 21.
11. Wright, introduction to *Black Metropolis*, xxxiii.
12. Davis, "Personal Elements in the Poetry of Phillis Wheatley," 192.
13. Flanzbaum, "Unprecedented Liberties: Re-Reading Phillis Wheatley," 78.
14. Flanzbaum, 78.
15. Wheatley also uses this stylistic choice in her poems "HYMN to the Morning" and "HYMN to the Evening."
16. West, *African Spirituality*, 38.
17. Mbiti notes that the "[s]unshine is one of the expressions of God's providence, as held by some peoples like the Akan, Ankore, Igbira, Kpelle and Ila. The sun appears every day, providing light, warmth, change of seasons and the growth of crops. . . . So the Akan call God 'the Shining One,' to signify that He is involved in the light of the celestial bodies whose shining symbolizes His presence in the universe . . . the people believe that God makes the sun to shine by day and the moon by night" (*African Religions and Philosophy* [Portsmouth, NH: Heinemann, 1969], 41). The sun tends to have similar qualities to those attributed to the Son of God, who is one with the Creator. This is significant because it further suggests Wheatley's familiarity with Christology upon her arrival on American shores.
18. Wheatley, "An HYMN to the Morning," pp. 56–57, line 17; Wheatley, "An HYMN to the Evening," pp. 58–59, lines 11–12.
19. Wheatley, "An Hymn to Humanity" in *Poems on Various Subjects*, pp. 96, lines 1–6.
20. Charles Wesley and John Wesley, "Hymn for Christmas-Day," verses 1–3.
21. Wesley, "Hymn for Christmas Day," verses 7–10.
22. Wheatley, "An Hymn to Humanity, p. 96, line 1.
23. Wheatley, "An Hymn to Humanity," p. 96, lines 25–30.
24. Wheatley, "An Hymn to Humanity," p. 95, line 3; p. 96, line 26.
25. Rev. 21:3 (KJV).
26. Wheatley, "An Hymn to Humanity," pp. 95–96, lines 7–18.
27. Wheatley, "An Hymn to Humanity," p. 95, lines 7–9.

28. Wheatley, "An Hymn to Humanity," p. 96, line 14.
29. Ps.119:71 (KJV).
30. Wheatley, "An Hymn to Humanity," p. 96, line 17.
31. Wheatley, "An Hymn to Humanity," p. 96, line 16.
32. Wheatley, "An Hymn to Humanity," p. 96, line 18.
33. Wheatley, "An Hymn to Humanity," p. 95, line 3.
34. Wheatley, "An Hymn to Humanity," p. 96, line 22.
35. My emphasis.
36. Armah, *The Eloquence of the Scribes*, 220.
37. Armah, 205.
38. Armah, 205.
39. Wheatley, "An Hymn to Humanity," p. 96, line 23.
40. Bercovitch, *The American Jeremiad*, 16.
41. Wheatley, "An Hymn to Humanity," p. 97, lines 31–36.

Chapter 5

Salvation Is Available

Thoughts on the Works of Providence

    ARISE, my soul, on wings enraptur'd, rise
    To praise the monarch of the earth and skies,
    Whose goodness and beneficence appear
    As round its centre moves the rolling year,
    Or when the morning glows with rosy charms,   5
    Or the sun slumbers in the ocean's arms:
    Of light divine be a rich portion lent
    To guide my soul, and favour my intent.
    Celestial muse, my arduous flight sustain,
    And raise my mind to a seraphic strain!   10

    Ador'd for ever be the God unseen,
    Which round the sun revolves this vast machine,
    Though to his eye its mass a point appears:
    Ador'd the God that whirls surrounding spheres,
    Which first ordain'd that mighty Sol should reign   15
    The peerless monarch of th' ethereal train:
    Of miles twice forty millions is his height,
    And yet his radiance dazzles mortal sight
    So far beneath—from him th' extended earth
    Vigour derives, and ev'ry flow'ry birth: 20
    Vast through her orb she moves with easy grace
    Around her Phœbus in unbounded space;
    True to her course th' impetuous storm derides,
    Triumphant o'er the winds, and surging tides.

    Almighty, in these wond'rous works of thine,   25
    What Pow'r, what Wisdom, and what Goodness shine?
    And are thy wonders, Lord, by men explor'd,
    And yet creating glory unador'd!

Creation smiles in various beauty gay,
While day to night, and night succeeds to day: 30
That Wisdom, which attends Jehovah's ways,
Shines most conspicuous in the solar rays:
Without them, destitute of heat and light,
This world would be the reign of endless night:
In their excess how would our race complain, 35
Abhorring life! how hate its length'ned chain!
From air adust what num'rous ills would rise?
What dire contagion taint the burning skies?
What pestilential vapours, fraught with death,
Would rise, and overspread the lands beneath? 40

Hail, smiling morn, that from the orient main
Ascending dost adorn the heav'nly plain!
So rich, so various are thy beauteous dies,
That spread through all the circuit of the skies,
That, full of thee, my soul in rapture soars, 45
And thy great God, the cause of all adores.

O'er beings infinite his love extends,
His Wisdom rules them, and his Pow'r defends.
When tasks diurnal tire the human frame,
The spirits faint, and dim the vital flame, 50
Then too that ever active bounty shines,
Which not infinity of space confines.
The sable veil, that Night in silence draws,
Conceals effects, but shews th' Almighty Cause;
Night seals in sleep the wide creation fair, 55
And all is peaceful but the brow of care.
Again, gay Phœbus, as the day before,
Wakes ev'ry eye, but what shall wake no more;
Again the face of nature is renew'd,
Which still appears harmonious, fair, and good. 60
May grateful strains salute the smiling morn,
Before its beams the eastern hills adorn!

Shall day to day and night to night conspire
To show the goodness of the Almighty Sire?
This mental voice shall man regardless hear, 65
And never, never raise the filial pray'r?
To-day, O hearken, nor your folly mourn

Salvation Is Available

For time mispent, that never will return.

But see the sons of vegetation rise,
And spread their leafy banners to the skies. 70
All-wise Almighty Providence we trace
In trees, and plants, and all the flow'ry race;
As clear as in the nobler frame of man,
All lovely copies of the Maker's plan.
The pow'r the same that forms a ray of light,   75
That call'd creation from eternal night.
"Let there be light," he said: from his profound
Old Chaos heard, and trembled at the sound:
Swift as the word, inspir'd by pow'r divine,
Behold the light around its maker shine,   80
The first fair product of th' omnific God,
And now through all his works diffus'd abroad.

As reason's pow'rs by day our God disclose,
So we may trace him in the night's repose:
Say what is sleep? and dreams how passing strange! 85
When action ceases, and ideas range
Licentious and unbounded o'er the plains,
Where Fancy's queen in giddy triumph reigns.
Hear in soft strains the dreaming lover sigh
To a kind fair, or rave in jealousy;   90
On pleasure now, and now on vengeance bent,
The lab'ring passions struggle for a vent.
What pow'r, O man! thy reason then restores,
So long suspended in nocturnal hours?
What secret hand returns the mental train,   95
And gives improv'd thine active pow'rs again?
From thee, O man, what gratitude should rise!
And, when from balmy sleep thou op'st thine eyes,
Let thy first thoughts be praises to the skies.
How merciful our God who thus imparts   100
O'erflowing tides of joy to human hearts,
When wants and woes might be our righteous lot,
Our God forgetting, by our God forgot!

Among the mental pow'rs a question rose,
"What most the image of th' Eternal shows?"   105
When thus to Reason (so let Fancy rove)

Her great companion spoke immortal Love.

"Say, mighty pow'r, how long shall strife prevail,
And with its murmurs load the whisp'ring gale?
Refer the cause to Recollection's shrine,   110
Who loud proclaims my origin divine,
The cause whence heav'n and earth began to be,
And is not man immortaliz'd by me?
Reason let this most causeless strife subside."
Thus Love pronounc'd, and Reason thus reply'd.   115

"Thy birth, celestial queen! 'tis mine to own,
In thee resplendent is the Godhead shown;
Thy words persuade, my soul enraptur'd feels
Resistless beauty which thy smile reveals."
Ardent she spoke, and, kindling at her charms,   120
She clasp'd the blooming goddess in her arms.

Infinite Love where'er we turn our eyes
Appears: this ev'ry creature's wants supplies;
This most is heard in Nature's constant voice,
This makes the morn, and this the eve rejoice;   125
This bids the fost'ring rains and dews descend
To nourish all, to serve one gen'ral end,
The good of man: yet man ungrateful pays
But little homage, and but little praise.
To him, whose works array'd with mercy shine,   130
What songs should rise, how constant, how divine![1]

"For God so loved the world, that he gave his only begotten Son, that whosoever believeth in him should not perish, but have everlasting life."

—John 3:16

"If the Son therefore shall make you free, ye shall be free indeed."

—John 8:36

A PROVIDENTIAL LIBERATION

A unique proposition arises upon encountering John 8:36. Suggestively, the evangelist places Jesus as the liberator of his people. The process of making one free is forceful, regardless of the method. So, Jesus goes about his liberative design by implicit force. His act brings with it permanence or at least undeniable change, for the formerly enslaved is now "free indeed." There is no doubt nor possibility of denial. Based on the context of this passage, freedom will come at a great cost to the divine liberator. The chains of bondage are not merely temporal; rather, the chains are the shackles of sin and the subjection thereof has distinctly spiritual implications. Ironically, Jesus is conversing with freed men who "were never in bondage to any man."[2] Hence, his assertion that they "shall know the truth, and the truth shall make "them" free is met with some confusion and disbelief.[3] Subsequently, Jesus expounds on his assertion, noting the difference between physical and spiritual freedom. They are presently committing sin and, by implication, are slaves to sin. Hence, they need to freely accept the invitation to be released from their constructed house of comfort to dwell in the presented liberator—a permanent dwelling.

In "Thoughts on the Works of Providence," Wheatley makes a similar assertion as Jesus in the previous passage coupled with an admonition for those who have determined to dwell within the houses they have constructed. She offers an olive branch from the "monarch of the earth and skies."[4] This extension of favor is no different than Jesus's offer of knowing the truth or God's offer in John 3:16 of access to a permanent dwelling through divine love. The dialogue Wheatley presents between Reason and Love artistically expresses the evangelist's conditional offer of divine knowledge in love. The first question that arises upon examining this poem is to what "works" is Wheatley referring, and how does Providence perform said works? Providence particularly seems to be a Calvinistic term and ideology, that God's primary operation within the world, particularly as it relates to human beings, is that of divine providence. It is the notion or belief that God provides for all creation, but his chosen peoples or promised people or elect people are set aside to be blessed and to inherit eternal life. Her thoughts, then, are her own interrogation and interpretation of how God interacts with humanity—her theology. This poetic theological exposition is important for Wheatley; it serves to set the tone and tenor of her subsequent and prior poetic articulations, pointing directly to this providential God as divine orchestrator and liberator.

The works of providence Wheatley engages either directly or indirectly combat various notions of divine right. Wheatley contends that the comfort and complacency within certain sects of the community has resulted in an inability to be faithful stewards of the benefits God has afforded humanity.

> Almighty, in these wond'rous works of thine,
> What Pow'r, what Wisdom, and what Goodness shine?
> And are thy wonders, Lord, by men explor'd,
> And yet creating glory unador'd![5]

The awesome nature of the "wond'rous works" are meant to be adored by all of creation. Wheatley systematically indicts those who have access to the tangible blessings of God as failing to be good stewards because of a refusal to simply adore God's creative glory.[6] She later returns to this notion suggesting that the ungrateful individual "pays / [b]ut little homage, and but little praise" to the creator God who consistently provides for humanity.[7]

The lack of appreciation is due to the assumption that the power of the human mind is equal with or greater than that of the divine. She appeals, as she often does, to the celestial muse to sustain her ascendency into the realm of the poet, to speak truth to power, to "raise [her] mind to a seraphic strain" because she understands, much like the prophet Isaiah, the futility of the human mind and voice.[8] Isaiah cries out to God, "Woe is me! for I am undone; because I am a man of unclean lips, and I dwell in the midst of a people of unclean lips: for mine eyes have seen the King, the Lord of hosts."[9] Isaiah knows his sinfulness "cannot be in the presence of God who is wholly pure, mighty, and set apart from all sin."[10] Wheatley, is hyperaware of the need for inspiration to write poetic verse in an influential and inspirational manner. By contrast, she implies at certain moments throughout the poem that her fellow white citizens seem not to hold the same view. The mind, in essence, is detached from the heart and soul of America. The danger of this detachment is that it reifies a lack of appreciation for God's providence on one hand and God's person on the other. According to Wheatley, it is God who provides an opening or "a vent" for the use of the human mind during the day.[11] The "active pow'rs" of the mind cannot be underappreciated;[12] however, if the mind refuses to send "praises to the skies" because of the "o'erflowing tides of joy to human hearts,"[13] it is as though reason has been promoted, thereby supplanting Love and Passion, without the acknowledging that the ability to reason is a gift.

It makes sense, then, that white Americans would view much of life through the lens of reason. "Excess" becomes the order of the day,[14] the striving of our dream—an American Dream. The American Dream is dripping with the residue of Manifest Destiny that fails to acknowledge the beauty in unity, all under the manufactured posture of divine right. The sublime is relegated to the possessors of people and reason. For this purpose, Wheatley artistically constructs a method to strategically reinject the community with a love and appreciation for the liberator God.

Wheatley opens the poem by talking to her soul, the essence of the self; then, she somewhat abruptly redirects her address toward the end of the first stanza by conjuring the "Celestial muse."[15] Though she seems to change the audience to whom she is addressing, she could be addressing a part of her being. Perhaps the Celestial muse resides within her soul. As a poet, her inspiration emanates from the muse who, much like the Holy Spirit, overshadows her in order to bring forth a newly conceived artistic articulation through poetry.[16] This artistic articulation will serve as her praise song[17] to the "monarch of the earth and skies."[18] It is as though her soulical identity is fluid with the "monarch" and "Celestial muse," meaning Wheatley views herself as a spiritual being, hence her language and juxtapositioning of addressees. By being in tune with this providential monarchal muse, she is not the master of her art or craft; rather, she is guided and favored to produce the artistic articulations that flow through her pen.[19] Her "seraphic strain" would be one,[20] thanks to the Celestial muse, directed to display a deep passion for this providential God. The seraphim traditionally are regarded as the heavenly beings that are particularly occupied with being zealous for God and creating an atmosphere that is intense and impassioned. The word literally means to burn with divine love. This is the intent of her articulations and, thereby, her theology. Her desire is to present a radical divine love that requires or warrants an equally impassioned love of humanity in order to create an atmosphere that is pleasant and acceptable to this providential monarchal muse, known as God.

Wheatley's praise song commences in the second stanza and continues resulting in a unique dialogue between higher beings that results in a deeper understanding of the inner workings of heavenly sphere. She commences her adulation noting how massive this God is, the creator God. In a sense, this poem serves as Wheatley's account of the creation. She notes that this massive God gives the "mighty *Sol*" dominion or reign of the "ethereal train."[21] The use of the Latin translation of sun is significant. Latin is the language of the papacy; it is the language used to order the worship experience in Roman Catholic services. Latin is the typical language used not only during worship but also in most official communiqués from the pope to certain regions of the Catholic constituency. In this way, her poem serves as a type of encyclical. The encyclical is a letter that is circulated. Most often, the contents instruct the church on different theological issues, particularly with regard to a new revelation or a call back to an original interpretation that has been abandoned through careless human activity. Thus, Wheatley reinterprets the "mighty Sol," the monarch of the skies. Particularly of note, she remains consistent in her use of the Latin, articulating the graceful dance between the earth and "her *Phoebus*."[22] Her use of the Latin name for the Greek god of the sun converges Eurocentric monotheistic notions onto the "accepted" polytheistic "historical" Greek mythology. Within an American or Western context, Greek mythology is considered an accepted and historically accurate component or worldview within the greater tapestry of the progression toward a Eurocentric monotheism. Readers of this poem would undoubtedly have little issue with her use of the Latin translation of the Greek god Apollo nor the appropriation of his function within the pantheon as a characteristic or attribute of the one and only God of the universe. Undoubtedly, the reception would be different if she would have incorporated the polytheistic understandings of Liza (Western Africa), Orunmila (Santeria), Ra (Egypt), or Utu (Mesopotamia), who are all considered types of sun gods who predate the universal Eurocentric concept of God. Wheatley's decision to merge the polytheistic and monotheistic understandings of the concept of God illumines her understanding of global religious practice as fluid, not needlessly held in unproductive, reductive tension. The Eurocentric methodology would be to present one religious belief system as dominant or more accurate. Her juxtaposition of these understandings serves as the underpinning for an approach to theology that can be potentially unifying.

Wheatley goes on to suggest that the sun is the source of power, wisdom, and goodness, which shine through and are evidently produced most effectively during the day. Yet, she notices an issue with the greatness of creation and particularly with the appreciation of the vastness of the wondrous created world. She notes humanity's inability to be faithful stewards of the various resources that we have access to: "And are thy wonders, Lord, by men explor'd, / And yet creating glory unador'd!"[23] It is as though men and women alike have taken the providence of God for granted. Particularly, she is possibly addressing the leaders of a new awakening in the American religious landscape, those reformers in the tradition of Luther, Calvin, and Zwingli. In particular, as suggested by the title of this poem, it would seem she is addressing those who theologically have Calvinist leanings. Knowing the sovereignty of God as creator, understanding the providence of God as divine architect and compass, and realizing the power of this almighty God, the Calvinist Christians ought to give consistent honor and glory to God who is their source. The created "wonders" of God are explored, examined, excavated, interpreted, and interrogated, yet these wonders are rarely appreciated for their worth. Giving glory or praise for the wonders of creation pleases God, so in Wheatley's current estimation, God is not fully pleased; subsequently, there is little peace throughout the world, particularly within America. Her justification for this idea is not unfounded, for in Luke chapter 2 the evangelist suggests that peace on earth and glory to God are related.[24] The peace God will bestow comes as a result of consistent glorification of God and no one or nothing else. Wheatley's mission is to articulate this and express it in a creative way. In this sense, she is the embodiment of what Emerson would later call "The Poet."

One of the reasons we as creation must consistently glorify God is due to God's consistent benefiting ways. She invokes for the first time the name "Jehovah" to express the tetragrammaton,[25] the unutterable. Her invocation of this name for God suggests that this god is not like any other deity and, hence, should be regarded as essential for life. The *"Wisdom, which attends Jehovah's ways,"*[26] is in no way comparable to any other source of wisdom. She likens it to the substance of the sun's rays. Wisdom is the essence of what guides us during the day; it is wisdom that provides the sight line to get us safely from one place to the next. In addition, this wisdom is what attends all of Jehovah's ways, meaning there is divine guidance available for all aspects of life's odyssey. Without Jehovah's wisdom-filled ways, "this world would be the reign of endless night."[27] Here, Wheatley is referencing the delivering as well as the guiding power of God. If the world would be "destitute of heat and light" if wisdom did not accompany Jehovah's ways,[28] then God's children would be captive to the darkness.[29] This time period is a dark season for America, in particular the slaveholding South, and Wheatley is attempting to provide a theological explanation of the condition of her people while simultaneously suggesting a paradigm for liberation that warrants an acknowledgment of the dangers of living without a complete understanding of the darkness and light.

Basking in the plenteous beneficence of the sun's rays, under the representation of the abiding presence of God, there is little justification for blacks in America to complain. Wheatley suggests, in the excess of wisdom, sunlight, knowledge, and growth and productivity, there is no need for "our race" to complain.[30] To the liberated conscience, life in America is a productive one. However, Wheatley seems to suggest that her race abhors life and its hateful chain that keeps black people in America bound. The irony lies in this chain of hate emanating from the beauty of creation. This chain is seemingly lengthened to restrict the movement of all who are not within the familial jurisdiction of the master's house.

Here, Harriett Jacobs lends some insight into the pervasiveness of the subordinating culture of the slavocracy, noting,

> Southern gentlemen indulge in the most contemptuous expressions about the Yankees, while they, on their part, consent to do the vilest work for them, such as the ferocious bloodhounds and the despised negro-hunters are employed to do at home. When southerners go to the north, they are proud to do them honor; but the northern man is not welcome south of Mason and Dixon's line, unless he suppresses every thought and feeling at variance with their "peculiar institution." Nor is it enough to be silent. The masters are not pleased, unless

they obtain a greater degree of subservience than that; and they are generally accommodated. Do they respect the northerner for this? I trow not. Even the slaves despise "a northern man with southern principles"; and that is the class they generally see. When northerners go to the south to reside, they prove very apt scholars. They soon imbibe the sentiments and disposition of their neighbors, and generally go beyond their teachers. Of the two, they are proverbially the hardest masters.

They seem to satisfy their consciences with the doctrine that God created the Africans to be slaves. What a libel upon the heavenly Father, who "made of one blood all nations of men!" And then who *are* Africans? Who can measure the amount of Anglo-Saxon blood coursing in the veins of American slaves?[31]

This point is also one of contention since the masters traditionally did not even accept those who were a part of their bloodline, their familial jurisdiction. So, within the construct of the slaveholding South, enslaved children of Euro-African descent could not claim the European part of their heritage and thereby were held captive and restricted by the same chain of hate. The innovation in this chain lies in the ability for it not only to be lengthened to ensnare the black bodies that were hated, but this chain can be lengthened, stretched out, reaffixed, and rekeyed in order to constrict any physical body, consciousness, or spirit. This chain of hate has been prevalent within American culture at least since the first settlers arrived on ships off the Atlantic coast because the chain is one of spiritual and ethical proportion. When physical restraint is needed, the chain is orchestrated as a physical restraint. When emotional or psychological captivity is desired, the chain is molded to fit the human psyche into a desired realm of possibility. This chain has been used throughout American history to restrict blacks, women, and ultimately anyone who fails to conform to the white hegemonic prescriptive for living. This is how "num'rous ills . . . rise" within American society.[32] Since the chain was formed as a psychosocial chain, it can be altered to reach and restrict anyone or anything the master deems a threat to his dominion over the land. For this reason, an expansion of the deep-seated hatred within whites is manifest seemingly "from [the] air" in the guise of a new law,[33] opinion, or system aimed at the restriction of a particular group. In this way, the overall hierarchy is maintained.

The "contagion" of hatred within America is so entrenched in the fabric of the society that it even taints "the burning skies."[34] The magnificence of the sun's rays, with its guiding and comforting qualities, is overpowered by this "dire contagion" that serves as an indelible mark of separation from the divine. Wheatley invokes the term "pestilential vapours" perhaps to allude to the plagues administered by God within the land of Egypt aimed at ridding the land of the Egyptian captors who had decided to view themselves as demagogues able to suppress and oppress other human beings. The spread of these poisonous vapors undoubtedly would cause suffocation and possible death. Since the statement is posed in the interrogative, the reader cannot but wonder if Wheatley is inquiring of God if God will cause an Egypt-like plague to "overspread the lands" such that the white slaveholders will be stricken and afflicted leaving the enslaved blacks in a position of promise with the help of an earthly liberator, a modern day Moses.[35] Her prescribed theology of liberation is rooted in biblical principles and allusions.

Amid this suppressing reality, the beauty of creation is able to break through if one is attentive, particularly early in the morning. The "smiling morn" is the embodiment of both the beauty and the purity of the created world.[36] Sunsets, though equally beautiful, are often tainted by the events of the day, but sunrises are innocently pure and representative of the ensuing opportunities of the newly promised day. Wheatley acknowledges the promises of the morning, with a direct connection to the direction or location of the rising son—the orient or the East. The natural sunrise is a blended reality, as articulated by Wheatley, "So rich, so various are thy beauteous dies, / that spread through all the circuit of the skies."[37] The created world is naturally designed to be inclusive of different colors that are rich in and of themselves yet have die-like qualities, meaning they can be mixed to create new colors while retaining components of their richness yet appearing as something new and different. This is what makes the morning unique and special for Wheatley. It is in the fullness of this type of beauty that she is completely freed from this life and taken away in a type of "rapture" moment, a moment when God and creation are in perfect harmony. Her deliverance, her liberation is only realized in this moment, a moment of full obedience by creation to the creator; this is a moment in which the creation adores God and God likewise adores creation in a similar fashion to her invocation earlier of the seraphim in the first stanza. Harmony and peace are the result of a proper orientation with regard to creator and creation.

This harmony is always imminent due to the expansiveness of God's love for creation. According to Wheatley, God's love knows no bounds, "O'er beings infinite his love extends. / His *Wisdom* rules them, and his *Pow'r* defends."[38] Because God loves "his" creation, God is a constant source of provision. Throughout the eighth stanza, Wheatley expresses a glimmer of hope against the backdrop of the harsh "tasks diurnal" that must be completed by those who are within the reach of the chains of hate.[39] She notes that even in the midst of such great strife and duress, God is faithful to God's creation; the "active bounty,"[40] the sun, still shines because it cannot be confined or restricted, as the black body can. It is in this moment that the "sable veil" of the *Night* draws in order to conceal the brutality of the day's activities.[41] The liberative move for Wheatley lies within this veil. Within the veil, the stories of the innumerable confined bodies are told. Within the veil, the praise songs are uplifted in code only deciphered by God. Within the veil, the promises of God are realized though the reality may still be contradictory. Within the veil, "the *Almighty Cause*" for liberation is exacted within the normalcy of the dance between day and night.[42]

Even amid the night, the providential God is ever watchful, waking everyone the next day except for those who "shall wake no more."[43] Again, the expectation is praise and adoration for extended providence. However, Wheatley seems to privilege anticipatory praise that rises "[b]efore [the sun's] beams the eastern hills adorn."[44] If humanity pays attention to the normalcy of day and night, if they would remain in tune with the ebb and flow of nature, they would witness the "goodness of the Almighty Sire."[45] It is imperative to live life to the fullest to make the most out of each opportunity. For Wheatley, this is how humanity renders an adequate response to the life-giving and life-sustaining God.

To seize the opportunity to persuade her captive audience, Wheatley recasts the Creation. The biblical account of the creation would have undoubtedly been a very familiar story for her readership. Her retelling, however, is not staid; rather, it is filled with personified imagery to pull the audience deeper into Wheatley's divinely orchestrated worldview. Chaos is personified in Wheatley's creation narrative. Though a mighty force, Chaos cowers at the voice of the Almighty God. Within creation, light is the first product of God. Light emerges out of darkness and despite the presence of Chaos. Darkness cannot effectively contend with light. This light is intended to spread, for it is "diffus'd abroad."[46] Wheatley recasts creation to get back to the original intent of God's creative acts. If light came first, light is preeminent and prevailing in and throughout all creation. There is no time nor space in which light is not acceptable and divinely expected to be present. Here, Wheatley is shifting between the historical and the metaphorical—a homiletical tool. Rodney Kennedy notes:

> Metaphor, as a creative power, is presented as the major component in a rhetoric of folly. Rather than view metaphor as an element of style, metaphor [can be resituated] as an element of rhetorical invention. Metaphor is capable of redescribing reality, producing a new world, and creating credibility, community, and concepts by which Christians and secularists structure reality.[47]

The creative function of the metaphor constructed by the poet-preacher is useful in the co-creating enterprise of which Wheatley is an instrument. Her job, as poet-preacher, is to be light, and, moreover, to be representative light, primed for imitation. Light is called out by God, as such, and is for God's use. Hence, if humanity is created by God, and light is created prior to

God's creation of humankind, then, humanity's first response to God should be to emit light. This light, however, seems to be absent or at least lacking in Wheatley's perceived world. Perhaps, if "Old *Chaos*" trembled in the beginning, Old Chaos can tremble and give way to light today. Wheatley uses "Old Chaos" as a figurative placeholder for all negative experiences and influences that have a "profound" effect and prominent position in our lives. Ironically, Chaos does not cease to exist with the creation of light; it is merely overtaken by the light.

After recasting this creation image, Wheatley shifts to speak to America's claimed seat of dominance—reason. Wheatley continues her analysis of American culture, noting the preeminence of reason and "the mental train."[48] It seems Wheatley is expressing her desire for those created in the image of God to reflect on what God has done, hence the need for God to disclose his acts so that we may reflect on them "by day."[49] The challenge is that "when action ceases," reason guides America down a "licentious and unbounded" path of imagination or "*Fancy*."[50] This path results in a vacillating damaging appropriation of love and respect, which is made manifest in America through the slavocracy. The deeply ensconced "lab'ring passions struggle for a vent" or an outlet of expression within an oppressive construct.[51] The result is an inability to see beyond the perverse creation of Reason. Wheatley acknowledges the potential and the problem:

> What pow'r, O man! thy reason then restores,
> So long suspended in nocturnal hours?
> What secret hand returns the mental train,
> And gives improv'd thine active pow'rs again?
> From thee, O man, what gratitude should rise!
> And, when from balmy sleep thou op'st thine eyes,
> Let thy first thoughts be praises to the skies.
> How merciful our God who thus imparts
> O'erflowing tides of joy to human hearts,
> When wants and woes might be our righteous lot,
> Our God forgetting, by our God forgot![52]

Reason seemingly is incapable of accessing and gaining the acceptance of the kingdom of God. Here, God's grace and sovereignty is presented as the only sustaining factor for a people consumed by reason. This becomes a prevailing motif in Wheatley's poetry—an inconsistently faithful people preserved by an immutably faithful God.

Throughout the poem, Wheatley gives voice to several aspects or realities within human life (in order of introduction): Sol, Phoebus, Power, Wisdom, Goodness, Jehovah, Night, Almighty Cause, Chaos, Fancy, Reason, Love, Recollection, and Nature. Each of these aspects is italicized in the original and authorized versions of Wheatley's poem. For this reason, the careful reader must ask, what is the poet-preacher's intent with usage and placement of these words and concepts. That there are fourteen takes us on a unique historical and conceptual journey. Sol, representing the Roman sun god, and Phoebus, representing the Greek god of the sun Apollo, coincide with Wheatley's discussion of and insistence on light in the poem. In addition, they lead the reader to reconceptualize the importance of light not only for biblical history but the ancient belief systems as well. This undoubtedly appeals to the philosophical and secular reader. Wheatley's use of Power, Wisdom, and Goodness bespeaks a trinity of the poet's creation that metaphorically represents the Holy Trinity. God the father as the representative of omnipotence, the Son as the representative of incomparable godly wisdom, and the Holy Spirit as the representative of goodness in the world. Simply, God as creator is all powerful, acceptance of Jesus as the son is considered a wise choice, and if you are in tune with the creator God, goodness emanates from your heart. This reading is supported with the insertion of Jehovah into the poem. Jehovah being the Latin derivative of YHWH serves as the supposed foundation for all English and thereby American conceptualizations of God and the Judeo-Christian religions. This introduction of Jehovah is ironically followed by the Night. Night has many representations: it could represent the intertestamental period within Christian traditions demarcating the silence of God. If this is true for the poet, it makes sense to appropriate a metaphorical understanding of the Night as a period of the inability of American slaveholders to hear the voice of God. Regardless, there is an Almighty Cause for the Night and ensuing Chaos. Though Chaos is suppressed with the creation, Chaos is still a reality for the enslaved African and rules the heart of the slave owner.

Upon Wheatley's assessment of Night, she introduces Fancy, Reason, and Love, who end up having a conversation that ushers the reader to Wheatley's summed up thoughts on the works of providence.

> Among the mental pow'rs a question rose,
> "What most the image of th' Eternal shows?"
> When thus to *Reason* (so let *Fancy* rove)
> Her great companion spoke immortal *Love*.

> "Say, mighty pow'r, how long shall strife prevail,
> And with its murmurs load the whisp'ring gale?
> Refer the cause to *Recollection's* shrine,
> Who loud proclaims my origin divine,
> The cause whence heav'n and earth began to be,
> And is not man immortaliz'd by me?
> *Reason* let this most causeless strife subside."

Thus *Love* pronounc'd, and *Reason* thus reply'd.

> "Thy birth, celestial queen! 'tis mine to own,
> In thee resplendent is the Godhead shown;
> Thy words persuade, my soul enraptur'd feels
> Resistless beauty which thy smile reveals."
> Ardent she spoke, and, kindling at her charms,
> She clasp'd the blooming goddess in her arms.[53]

As a bystander overhearing this conversation among the heavenly beings, the "mental pow'rs," Wheatley recounts what the muses have enabled her to hear. The question that emerges is one of divine proportions. In essence, what is the dominant image of God? Or, what or who best represents God? Reason is then addressed by Love. Interestingly, Fancy is dismissed as a wanderer. Love begins to speak for the first time, noting the strife of the current moment as overwhelming and irritating storm winds. Love continues, petitioning to Reason to confer with Recollection to determine the origin of the current chaos and how the "cause whence heav'n and earth began to be" is directly connected to the present predicament. Love concludes by laying the power to end the "causeless strife" with Reason. Reason replies that the current strife is borne of Reason, and Love is the resplendent representative of the Godhead. It is here that we see the embrace of Reason and Love, "[s]he clasp'd the blooming goddess in her arms." Love's blooming suggests that the realization of a new way of love is new.

Though the awareness of Love is new, Love is herself infinite. Wheatley arrives at the conclusion that the providence of God is represented in the love of God. And that conceptualization of love is most liberating. When looking at the world through the lens of love, newness emerges, as well as a greater appreciation for the providence of God. It is love that supplies every creature's wants. It is love that is "heard in *Nature's* constant voice." It is love that ushers in the morning. It is love that makes the "eve rejoice"; Love commences the rains and dew to nourish the world and serve one end: the good of man.[54] An awareness of love encourages humanity to point to a creator God, a liberator God, and a lovecentric God to offer praise. Praise is the appropriate response to a God of divine providence. What songs should rise out of the hearts of humanity? Perhaps it is the praise songs of the slaves that recognize the love of God despite the reality of seemingly ceaseless chaotic night:

> When Israel was in Egyptland,
> Let my people go,
> Oppressed so hard they could not stand,
> Let my people go.

> Go down, Moses,
> Way down in Egyptland,
> Tell old Pharaoh,
> "Let my people go."
>
> "Thus saith the Lord," bold Moses said,
> "Let my people go,
> If not, I'll smite your first-born dead,
> Let my people go.
>
> "No more shall they in bondage toil,
> Let my people go,
> Let them come out with Egypt's spoil,
> Let my people go."[55]

Or perhaps the anticipatory cadence of the melodic retelling of Daniel's deliverance serves as a sustaining refrain:

> Didn't my Lord deliver Daniel
> Deliver Daniel, deliver Daniel?
> Didn't my Lord deliver Daniel?
> An' why not-a every man?
>
> He delivered Daniel from de lion's den,
> Jonah from de belly of de whale.
> An' de Hebrew chillun from de fiery furnace,
> An' why not every man?
>
> I set my foot on de Gospel ship,
> An' de ship begin to sail.
> It landed me over on Canaan's shore
> An' I'll never come back no mo'
>
> Didn't my Lord deliver Daniel
> Deliver Daniel, deliver Daniel?
> Didn't my Lord deliver Daniel?
> An' why not-a every man?[56]

Wheatley consistently affirms that perseverance is an innate characteristic of the oppressed. Through perseverance and the commitment of divine help, a better day is on the horizon, and liberation reigns. This is the message that must be shared with burgeoning minds to shape the future trajectory of humanity.

WHEATLEY ON STAGE

To the University of Cambridge, in New England

> WHILE an intrinsic ardor prompts to write,
> The muses promise to assist my pen;
> 'Twas not long since I left my native shore
> The land of errors, and Egyptian gloom:
> Father of mercy, 'twas thy gracious hand   5
> Brought me in safety from those dark abodes.
>
> Students, to you 'tis giv'n to scan the heights
> Above, to traverse the ethereal space,
> And mark the systems of revolving worlds.
> Still more, ye sons of science ye receive   10
> The blissful news by messengers from heav'n,
> How Jesus' blood for your redemption flows.
> See him with hands out-stretcht upon the cross;
> Immense compassion in his bosom glows;
> He hears revilers, nor resents their scorn: 15
> What matchless mercy in the Son of God!
> When the whole human race by sin had fall'n,
> He deign'd to die that they might rise again,
> And share with him in the sublimest skies,
> Life without death, and glory without end.   20
>
> Improve your privileges while they stay,
> Ye pupils, and each hour redeem, that bears
> Or good or bad report of you to heav'n.
> Let sin, that baneful evil to the soul,
> By you be shunn'd, nor once remit your guard;   25
> Suppress the deadly serpent in its egg.
> Ye blooming plants of human race divine,
> An Ethiop tells you 'tis your greatest foe;
> Its transient sweetness turns to endless pain,
> And in immense perdition sinks the soul.[57]   30

The stage is set. The chairs are lined in formation with the appropriate distance for visual effect and processional facility. Can you hear the band members playing the processional song as the sun is rising on the campus quadrangle? It is in this moment that the dignitaries and administrators of the University of Cambridge take the stage, and the students begin to process in. Perhaps some of the students are slightly perplexed by the makeup of the dais, for, on stage, there is a young black girl, nearly the same age as the graduating class, who has been invited to speak. Phillis Wheatley is this young black girl, and she chooses to seize the opportunity by engaging her prophetic poetic imagination while on stage, in clear view and earshot of the eager graduating class.

As a type of preacher/prophet, Wheatley uses the trope of the biblical creation account and subsequent fall to admonish the students at Cambridge University and to encourage them to seek an alternative "foundation" intellectually, socioeconomically, and ethically. She attempts to expose the duality of knowledge to them. Knowledge is used to introduce sin on the one hand and to cure it on the other hand. By engaging foundational aspects of the doctrine of creation, Wheatley juxtaposes a created America (in its uniqueness) and the created world. In essence, America proves to be a corrupt expression of divine intent. The corrupt nature of sin, pervasiveness of unchecked evil, and the ability of humanity to serve as a host proves to be America's greatest flaw. Sin, as a foreign agent, is introduced first to the mind, then to the body, resulting in an unethical lived experience.

Creation in "To the University of Cambridge"

"To the University of Cambridge" provides an example of Wheatley's awareness of the way creation doctrine informs theology at its most basic level. In the biblical creation account, God orders the chaos of the "formless void" to commence the creative act. Upon creating human beings in the image of God, God instructs Adam and Eve, the representatives of humankind, to avoid eating from the "tree of the knowledge of good and evil . . . for in the day that thou eatest thereof thou shalt surely die."[58] All of creation, including Adam and Eve, is in order and compliant with all the commands of God until the serpent or fallen angel enters as a tempter, enticing humankind with godly privileges, especially knowledge, which he claims differentiates God from humans: "You shall not surely die: For God doth know that in the day ye eat thereof, then your eyes shall be opened, and ye shall be as gods, knowing good and evil."[59] In the Genesis creation account, the "deadly serpent" is not suppressed in its egg.[60] So, Adam and Eve cannot resist the temptation of being like God. Their failure becomes a warning to the students to whom she addresses in this poem.

Salvation Is Available   95

"To the University of Cambridge" functions as a kind of jeremiad that extends the serpent metaphor as Wheatley encourages the students to decide differently and reject sin outright. In this case, sin is slavery, and the claim to divine right emerges to justify the original sin. Addressing the graduating students at Cambridge, Wheatley implores them to take advantage of the opportunities afforded them for the sake of the future success of America. Stanza 3 calls attention to creation mythology in its allusions to the Garden of Eden:

> Improve your privileges while they stay,
> Ye pupils, and each hour redeem, that bears
> Or good or bad report of you to heav'n.
> Let sin, that baneful evil to the soul,
> By you be shunn'd, not once remit your guard;
> Suppress the deadly serpent in its egg.
> Ye blooming plants of human race divine,
> An *Ethiop* tells you tis your greatest foe;
> Its transient sweetness turns to endless pain,
> And in immense perdition sinks the soul.[61]

The students Wheatley addresses are in pursuit of knowledge just as Eve and Adam were in pursuit of knowledge. Sin entered the world through a quest for knowledge (fruit from the tree of the knowledge of good and evil according to Genesis 2:9), and Wheatley suggests that the pursuit of knowledge eradicates sin. Her choice to address these students, then, could prompt an unconventional use of this knowledge resulting in the removal of sin.

In the above lines, Wheatley re-creates a type of Eden, which cannot be interpreted in isolation from the fall of man, and she invokes foundational concepts that inform the doctrine of creation—namely sin, evil, and humanity. The beauty of Eden exists despite the sinful, fallen state of humanity. Her framework does not privilege arguments that human equality became problematized during the biblical Exodus. Harkening back to the original sin, she describes sin as the "baneful evil of the soul."[62] Her assessment is that sin corrupts individuals at their core, so every effort must be made to avoid it. The students must capitalize on their privilege to study and vigilantly guard against sin, which has the tendency to become all consuming. It is not that knowledge leads to less sin but that they should use their knowledge to see sin in humanity and help prevent it from consuming those around them. Wheatley further alludes to the fact that sin does not necessarily enter from within humanity. Rather, it is introduced by something external. Her use of the image of the deadly serpent, which is representative of evil in the doctrine of creation, conveys her understanding of how sin enters the world. The deadly serpent introduces sin, so the serpent must be crushed in its embryonic state or early stages. The students, in other words, must not perpetuate the sinful ways of their forefathers, namely enslavement of other humans. They must crush any sympathetic understanding or endorsement of a potential capitalistic enterprise of enslavement—America's original sin—before it becomes the endless pain to which she alludes in the subsequent lines. Noting their culpability and predisposition for agency as "privileged" pupils capable of eradicating this abomination, she encourages these students, blooming plants in the Garden of Eden, to restore the created order of things. In the beginning, when God created the world and everything in it, God created one human race, equal in significance. Through the fall to sin, that standard of equality was altered with individual perceptions taking precedence over God's intended perception. She writes against the common discourse about black humanity, namely, that black people are incapable of being fully human. By presenting this argument through the lens and language of creation, she actually suggests that slavery is not the lone source of black people's plight. The source is attended by a corrupt ethic that results in the unequal treatment of certain people. She is using perception and possession as the foci for articulating her corrective to restore the created order of things. It is in this Garden of Eden that Adam and Eve come to the awareness that they are naked after falling and receiving worldly knowledge. This is a part of the creation myth Wheatley seeks to combat. It is due to the fallen state of white America that Wheatley writes to these students, referring to them as blooming plants, in hopes that they might be able to rediscover the original intent of their existence and opportunities, thereby responding correctly to God's creative act.

Notably, Wheatley describes herself as an "Ethiop" in the lines that overtly warn the students of the consequences of a soul-defining misstep. As she asserts her credibility as one who is able to understand the things of God's creation, she also asserts an African authority or interpretation of Christian doctrine. If an Ethiop, one from an uncivilized or savage background, is aware, then surely these "brilliant" students should be aware of the evils of sin. Her role is to warn the students of the implications of their sin as heirs of the enslaving class. In this sense, she is operating as a prophet of Christ figure called by God to sound the alarm letting the people of God know that the current path they are on leads to destruction.

In an earlier manuscript of the same poem, Wheatley more explicitly engages the evil of slavery in America as a corrupted expression of the created order of things. As James Levernier notes, there is a possibility that the "'error's darkest night' that Wheatley witnessed in Africa was not the evils of paganism . . . but the unspeakable evils of slavers, who violated the natural rights of innocent natives by stealing them from their families, wantonly abusing them aboard ship, and then selling them into perpetual bondage."[63] His analysis stems from Lynn Matson's comparative analysis of the third stanza of "Cambridge" between the manuscript version and the published version. The published version replaces the word "sin" in line 24 with "hateful vice" and "deadly serpent" in line 26 with "sable monster." Though Matson's argument is that Wheatley's editorial choices are primarily changes in the tone to make it "milder,"[64] Wheatley's editorial changes in this instance may have actually assisted in identifying theological problems within American society. The manuscript version's use of "hateful vice" undoubtedly points to the morally corrupt slave system that serves as the true weakness of American civilization. The change protects Wheatley from being accused of unlawfully speaking out against slavery; but the change also exposes, artistically so, the root cause of the immoral behaviors—sin, not as an act but as a state of being.[65] If the "vice" can be avoided or shunned, the "sin" remains, and the vice or habit soon resurfaces. But if the "sin" is avoided or shunned, the "vice" ceases to exist because the sin, an individual's nature, is the root of the vice. Likewise, Wheatley's decision to substitute "Suppress the sable monster in its growth" with "Suppress the deadly serpent in its egg" demonstrates her awareness of the relation of creation to human behavior. In the Christian creation myth, the serpent is a fallen angel, once a part of the divine order but no longer favored because of its action.[66] The change from "the sable monster," which could refer to slavery, to "the deadly serpent" signals a shift from the institution to those who uphold it. The sin, if suppressed, can be avoided in any instance. But only the final line speaks to equality among the divine as a principle of creation. Regardless of Wheatley's rationale for making these editorial changes, the changes she makes help to call attention to the theological stance with regard to creation and restoring the original intent of divine creation.

Again, using the duality of knowledge acquisition, Wheatley presses her claim further by arguing for a reconceptualization of what atonement means. Salvation, like sin, is not necessarily a one-time act; rather, it, too, is a state of being. Redemption, forgiveness, and restoration are all available through the rightly appropriated knowledge of salvation. As Wheatley presents it, American cultural advancement is reliant on these "sons of science" living into a type of salvation that replaces divine right resulting in a newly created culture,[67] a culture that is humane and diverse.

Salvation in "To the University of Cambridge"

The understanding of salvation as an impartial pardon was not readily accepted in the manner I suggest Wheatley uses it. She is not merely stating Christ dies for all, thereby giving them access to salvation; she is also suggesting that a second salvation is available to and sometimes necessary for the so-called saved or Christians. This speaks to the progressive work of the atonement, namely, that salvation is something that is both realized and experienced. The new convert may have come to the realization of salvation or awareness of salvation, but the experience of salvation is what follows in a progressive manner such that your awareness deepens as the newfound relationship continues. She suggests a need for the white people in particular to be saved a second time because the first one was not taken seriously or at least coopted by the slavery enterprise resulting in the enslavers living a contradictory life. She expresses a basic articulation of what this type of salvation is and its cultural import to the graduating students in lines 10 through 20 of "To the University of Cambridge":

> Still more, ye sons of science ye receive
> The blissful news by messengers from heav'n,
> How *Jesus'* blood for your redemption flows.
> See him with hands out-stretcht upon the cross;
> Immense compassion in his bosom glows;
> He hears revilers, nor resents their scorn:
> What matchless mercy in the Son of God!
> When the whole human race by sin had fall'n,
> He deign'd to die that they might rise again,
> And share with him in the sublimest skies,
> Life without death, and glory without end.[68]

Amid the Enlightenment age and the suggestive exactness of science, Wheatley urges the students to allow their minds to conceive a heavenly report.[69] She frames her plea within the constructs of their academic worldview, noting that she understands they are the "sons of science," the developing possessors of worldly knowledge. These students are the ones who will frame the socioeconomic landscape in the decades to come; they are the future of America. Wheatley juxtaposes bliss with science to substantiate her claims and discourse, for she does not approach them as peer or fellow scholar. Rather, she approaches them as possessor and proclaimer of a heavenly message that Jesus died for their redemption.[70]

My earlier analysis of Wheatley's multiple versions of lines 34 through 37 of "On the Death of Rev. Mr. George Whitefield" in chapter 2 helps to elucidate her message in line 12 of "To the University of Cambridge." The flowing blood of redemption is connected directly to the "life-giving stream" and "fountain of redeeming blood" in her poetic memoir of Whitefield.[71] The earlier version of that poem, which Matson and Harris highlight, is "Grace's Heavenly Road."[72] As such, the impartial pardon emerges yet again as synonymous with Wheatley's understanding of grace. Her argument here is that these "sons of science" have a unique opportunity to experience transformation and receive this second, progressive, salvation before attaining positions of power and authority that the generation before them currently inhabit.

She vividly paints the picture of Jesus's crucifixion, imploring the young scholars to visualize "him with hands out-stretcht upon the cross."[73] She accents his compassion amidst reviling and scorn. In this moment, she seems to be referring directly to Luke 23:34 and Luke 23:43 where Jesus comments: "Father, forgive them, for they know not what they do."[74] Jesus is suggesting that the scribes, Pharisees, kings, and citizens who have facilitated this sentence of death by crucifixion do not fully understand what they have done. It is in this moment that Jesus shifts his focus stating, "Verily I say unto thee, To day shalt thou be with me in paradise."[75] He no longer talks with his father nor about those who have put him on the cross. He actually addresses one of the thieves who is being crucified with him. He lets the thief know that even though he is considered a vagabond, an outsider, and a sinner, he, too, has access to paradise through the shed blood of Jesus. Wheatley uses the scene of Jesus at Calvary to represent his ability to forgive, redeem, and restore all amid persecution and his ability to extend pardon specifically to the students who represent the future of the white, slaveholding race.

In addition, her directive to "look at him" could be a plea for them to look at what and who Jesus represents. First, Jesus represents the wrongfully accused, those who find themselves looking in the face of accusers who base their judgments on the assumption that difference suggests fault. Second, Wheatley wants these students to look at Jesus, an acceptable representative, and thereby look at her as a conduit for the restoration of a corrupt American culture. Wheatley is living into the prophetic tradition by "speaking truth to power" to incite radical transgressive action that is founded upon solid moral principles.

She makes the claim to the students that some things in life are heart acts and not head acts, for "immense compassion in his bosom glows."[76] Jesus does not primarily act with his head knowledge of people and their circumstances because "the Lord seeth not as man seeth; for man looketh on the outward appearance, but the Lord looketh on the heart."[77] Wheatley articulates several messages at once: Redemption is available to these white students; forgiveness is available for the white people who have wronged black people and the black people who psychologically have been coerced into thinking they have committed some crime; and restoration is available to black people who have been outcast and displaced from their positions within the fabric of humanity. In addition, restoration is available retroactively to the slaveholding generation through these "sons of science." This means the action she is promoting—the decision to accept the "matchless mercy in the Son of God"—though seemingly illogical, is necessary for American cultural advancement. After describing the events of Calvary and the importance of accepting the grace extended there, Wheatley briefly discusses the consequence of Calvary—eternal life. It is significant to note her use of both the sublime and glory to articulate how life triumphs over death. Through the crucifixion, Jesus reclaims the "whole human race" that had fallen or died due to original sin.[78] It was necessary, then, for Jesus to die to redeem the human race, yet it was also necessary for the resurrection to occur because his resurrection represents the resurrection of fallen humanity. Salvation proves essential for Wheatley in this poem because it precedes her discussion of Creation and the fall, setting up a Christocentric doctrine of creation. Her discussion of salvation displays her understanding of the nature of humanity and the possibility of redemption.

Significantly, Wheatley asserts that Christ's salvific act is both an act of grace and mercy in line 16. The nuance is meaningful because mercy is protective whereas grace is promotive. She suggests that the only way for these "sons of science" to avoid living into the heretical Christian praxis of their forefathers is through an authentic acceptance of the "matchless mercy" in Jesus Christ. Wheatley expresses that a shared experience of grace or "glory without end" is available to these students if they participate in and accept the preventive restorative redemption offered at Calvary.[79] What results is a nonbiased, nondistinct salvation that cancels out divine right. The students are "To day" or "this day" presented with a transgressive understanding of salvation that resists binaries within normative Christian understanding and practice.[80]

To date, few scholars have interrogated Wheatley's "To the University of Cambridge" giving consideration to the development of a salvation theory with the exception of Mary McAleer Balkun, who presents Wheatley as a preacher and the platform at the University of Cambridge as her pulpit. Noting the prevalence of the Puritan tradition, Balkun suggests that Wheatley understood that words could lead to redemption. This was a traditional Puritan belief; the preacher's words could actually affect the hearer such that the hearer's perception would be altered. Balkun continues, noting Wheatley's use of imagery and allusions within the structure of the poem to assist in the process of altering her "audience's system of reference and, as a result, its perceptions."[81] Wheatley's personal redemption results in her words being vouchsafed to such a degree that her audience will not question her authority because, based on the language of the poem, her authority comes directly from God. Interestingly, Balkun displaces Jesus within her analysis of Wheatley's engagement with the events at Calvary, particularly with regard to Jesus's acts of compassion, preferring to place Wheatley in that position as the one holding "no grudge toward her revilers."[82] Significantly, her decision to place Wheatley on the cross enables her to stress Wheatley's "unwillingness to cast herself overtly as one of the saved—her use of *they* rather than *we*—underscores the subtlety of the mind at work in these lines and its awareness of the audience to which it is appealing. It also underscores her personal lesson of Christian humility and generosity."[83] In addition, this position undergirds Wheatley's understanding of community and the need for a common understanding of the essence of what makes a person a part of humanity. Wheatley seemingly detaches herself from humanity for a moment, showing how Jesus Christ completed the salvific work at Calvary. He had to empty himself of his divinity to enter this world, and he had to sacrifice his human nature to fulfill the promise of resurrection, redemption, and restoration to fallen humanity: "He deign'd to die that they might rise again."[84] Significant here, however, is the need to engage the racial tensions in the text, namely that Wheatley is addressing an all-white, all male "congregation." Thus, Wheatley's sermon does more than simply address the possibility of resurrection, redemption, and restoration for fallen humanity. She creatively presents these white "sons of science" with a nonnormative preventive prescription of access to an authentic/democratic salvation that, upon receipt, will assist in the ultimate resurrection of American culture. This poetic sermon serves as Wheatley's invitation for this generation to resist the sin of their fathers "this day" to help the "Ethiop" and the darker people in America gain their freedom while simultaneously restoring communal relations as articulated by Jesus on the cross.[85]

The restoration of communal relations is significant for Wheatley because of her belief that, according to divine creation, we are called to live in community. M. Shawn Copeland asserts, "Black theology strives to discern, understand, interpret, and impart the word of God and its meaning for the historical, religious, cultural, and social life of the Black community."[86] Though black theology as a type of liberation theology is typically framed in a unifocal manner—that is, for the black community—Wheatley clearly extends the understanding/parameters of liberation theology by consistently assessing American culture throughout her poetry. She identifies slavery in America as a corrupted expression of the created order of things, dismissing the divinely orchestrated equality of human personality. In Genesis 1:26a, God shaped humankind "in our image, after our likeness" for the sake of cultural stability. God's initial creation was one of equality and communal respect. Wheatley asserts that America has deviated from the original intent because of sin, "that baneful evil of the soul."[87] The sin manifest in America enters by the "serpent," an outside source of evil, and, like the biblical account, corrupts the divinely designed social order, which serves as the foundation for Wheatley's call for a theology of liberation. Sin is the primary force Wheatley seeks to combat. In her development of a liberation theology, sin "is reflected on not merely through individual moral acts or existential separation and despair, but primarily in terms of social structures."[88] Since Wheatley's understanding of sin is social, the solution must have social implications as well.

Based on Wheatley's approach and the reality of a sin sick America, liberation has to emerge out of the imagination. The historical Christ has died and is no longer physically in the world to initiate some type of revolution; thus Wheatley must do so. The imagination for Wheatley is the thread that connects the Christian of the eighteenth century to the Christ of antiquity. The Apostle Paul states, "Let this mind be in you, which was also in Christ Jesus."[89] The mind of Christ is a creative one as reflected in the creation narrative articulated by Wheatley in "On Imagination," which I address in the next chapter. Hence, the imagination must be reflexive in nature. Not only must we possess an imagination; the imagination must possess us. This reflexive possession results in transformative liberation. For Wheatley, Christ represents the conduit for all transformation—body, mind, and soul. Common representations of Christ within the discourse of liberation theology support her view. Christ is typically understood as "[the] political rebel, . . . [the one] suffering as the scourged of the earth, . . . [and as being] in solidarity with the poor and oppressed—Christ as liberator, as one who actually effects transformation, as one who brings new ways of being human."[90] Wheatley's appropriation of a reflexive imagination is what enables her liberation theology to reach beyond the bounds of race to provide a viable approach to cultural improvement.

Wheatley recognizes a need for a new creation, an alternate reality, particularly for black people in America. However, realizing the uplift of the black race cannot be achieved in a vacuum, she integrates it with her understanding of salvation or soteriology, what might be called her "democratic" understanding of salvation or redemption, meaning she suggests a salvation that is equally available to black people and white people in America. The redemptive flow of Christ's blood is available and potent enough to claim "pagans" and reclaim Christians. The unbeliever is now granted access to "glory without end,"[91] and the believer who has been enamored and imprisoned by the enslavement-promoting and separatist mongering serpent can now be readmitted through renewal. Based on Wheatley's assertions, this dual understanding of salvation results in cultural improvement—a new American reality, which is really a return to God's original intent for humanity. Her theology seeks to liberate black people and white people simultaneously. She realizes that the black body, mind, and soul must be liberated in community because black bodies, minds, and souls are inextricably connected to white bodies, minds, and souls. Her desire is for a universal liberation—a true redemption—that is culturally accountable and sustainable.

NOTES

1. Wheatley, "Thoughts on the Work of Providence," in *Poems on Various Subjects*, pp. 43–50, lines 1–31.
2. Jn. 8:33 (KJV); The irony of this claim is notable. As descendants of Abraham, these Israelites are in the genealogical line of Isaac, Jacob, and Judah and his brothers. Hence, they are descendants of those who were in Egyptian captivity as slaves for some four hundred years prior to the Exodus.
3. Jn. 8:32 (KJV).
4. Wheatley, "Thoughts on the Works of Providence," p. 43, line 2.
5. Wheatley, "Thoughts on the Works of Providence," p. 44, lines 25–28.
6. This is a frequent refrain of Wheatley's. We see it in "To the University of Cambridge" as well. She has a deep desire to see people using the gifts, opportunities, statuses, privileges afforded them for the benefit of the masses. Her social justice bent is prevailing throughout her poetry, clearly defining her as a prophetic preacher-poet.
7. Wheatley, "Thoughts on the Works of Providence," p. 44, lines 28–29.
8. Wheatley, "Thoughts on the Works of Providence," p. 43, line 10.
9. Is. 6:5 (KJV).
10. Jusu, *Africa Study Bible*, 991.
11. Wheatley, "Thoughts on the Works of Providence," p. 47, line 92.
12. Wheatley, "Thoughts on the Works of Providence," p. 48, line 96.
13. Wheatley, "Thoughts on the Works of Providence," p. 48, line 99, 101.
14. Wheatley, "Thoughts on the Works of Providence," p. 45, line 35.
15. Wheatley, "Thoughts on the Works of Providence," p. 43, line 9.
16. Lk. 1:35 (KJV).
17. Luke 1:46–56. Here, Mary, the mother of Jesus of Nazareth, sings praises to God for favoring her to carry the son of God. She ties her praise song to the narrative of the people of Israel, making her exuberation both historical and theological. She finds joy in knowing that God had selected her for such a task and responsibility despite her low estate by society's estimation. Her song directly pays homage to the sovereignty of God, particularly as it relates to God's providence, for the praise song articulated by Mary, according to most new testament scholars, is the fulfillment of several old testament prophecies.
18. Wheatley, "Thoughts on the Works of Providence," p. 43, line 2.
19. Wheatley, "Thoughts on the Works of Providence," p. 43, line 8.
20. Wheatley, "Thoughts on the Works of Providence," p. 43, line 10.
21. Wheatley, "Thoughts on the Works of Providence," p. 43, line 15–16.
22. Wheatley, "Thoughts on the Works of Providence," p. 44, lines 21–22.
23. Wheatley, "Thoughts on the Works of Providence," p. 44, lines 27–28.
24. Luke 2:8–21 recounts the birth of Jesus Christ with special emphasis on the response of those who subscribe to a belief in God when presented with the gift, "wonder," provision that is the baby called Jesus who is born in the ghetto of Bethlehem. Particularly in the Holman Christian Standard translation verse 14 notes, "Glory to God in the highest heaven, and peace on earth to people He favors." The significance is that Mary as favored is favored because of her desire to please God,

which is manifest through her glorifying God through both her rhetoric and her actions. Mary's articulation of glorification is found in her praise song (Lk. 1:46–56), and her activation of glorification is found in her faithful and sacrificial obedience to the will of God.

25. YHWH (Yaweh) in Hebrew has no vowel points and, therefore, is inarticulate. Jehovah is the Latin translation of this Hebrew name for God. The tetragrammaton refers to the most accurate description of the personhood of God, "I am who I am" (Ex. 3:14).
26. Wheatley, "Thoughts on the Works of Providence," p. 44, line 31.
27. Wheatley, "Thoughts on the Works of Providence," p. 44, line 34.
28. Wheatley, "Thoughts on the Works of Providence," p. 44, line 33.
29. Ex. 13:21–22.
30. Wheatley, "Thoughts on the Works of Providence," p. 45, line 35.
31. Jacobs, *Incidents,* 55–56.
32. Wheatley, "Thoughts on the Works of Providence," p. 45, line 37.
33. Wheatley, "Thoughts on the Works of Providence," p. 45, line 37.
34. Wheatley, "Thoughts on the Works of Providence," p. 45, line 38.
35. Wheatley, "Thoughts on the Works of Providence," p. 45, line 40.
36. Wheatley, "Thoughts on the Works of Providence," p. 45, line 41.
37. Wheatley, "Thoughts on the Works of Providence," p. 45, lines 43–44.
38. Wheatley, "Thoughts on the Works of Providence," p. 45, lines 47–48.
39. Wheatley, "Thoughts on the Works of Providence," p. 45, line 49.
40. Wheatley, "Thoughts on the Works of Providence," p. 45, line 51.
41. Wheatley, "Thoughts on the Works of Providence," p. 45, line 53.
42. Wheatley, "Thoughts on the Works of Providence," p. 45, line 54.
43. Wheatley, "Thoughts on the Works of Providence," p. 46, line 58.
44. Wheatley, "Thoughts on the Works of Providence," p. 46, line 62.
45. Wheatley, "Thoughts on the Works of Providence," p. 46, line 64.
46. Wheatley, "Thoughts on the Works of Providence," p. 47, line 82.
47. Kennedy, "The Epistemic Power of Metaphor," vi.
48. Wheatley, "Thoughts on the Works of Providence," p. 48, line 95.
49. Wheatley, "Thoughts on the Works of Providence," p. 47, line 83.
50. Wheatley, "Thoughts on the Works of Providence," p. 47, lines 86–88.
51. Wheatley, "Thoughts on the Works of Providence," p. 47, line 92.
52. Wheatley, "Thoughts on the Works of Providence," pp. 47–48, lines 93–103.
53. Wheatley, "Thoughts on the Works of Providence," pp. 48–49, lines 104–121.
54. Wheatley, "Thoughts on the Works of Providence," pp. 49–50, lines 124–128.
55. "Go Down Moses," in *Norton Anthology of African American Literature,* 14–15.
56. "Didn't My Lord Deliver Daniel?" in *Norton Anthology of African American Literature,* 17–18.
57. Wheatley, "To the University of Cambridge, in New England" in *Poems on Various Subjects,* pp. 15–16, lines 1–30.
58. Gen. 2:17 (KJV).
59. Gen. 3:4–5 (KJV).
60. Wheatley, "To the University of Cambridge," p. 16, line 26.

61. Wheatley, "To the University of Cambridge," p. 16, lines 21–30.
62. Wheatley, "To the University of Cambridge," p. 16, line 24.
63. Levernier, "Style as Protest," 177.
64. Matson, "Phillis Wheatley—Soul Sister?," 229.
65. Wayne Grudem (*Systematic Theology: An Introduction to Biblical Doctrine* [Grand Rapids: Zondervan. 2000]) notes that "sin is any failure to conform to the moral law of God in act, attitude, or nature" (490). The inability to control one's sinful nature results in total depravity, which occurs when "every part of our being is affected by sin" (497). This manifests itself through our intellects, thoughts, desires, and emotions. Ultimately, this sin infection grips our hearts, controlling our motivations, goals, aspirations, and actions (497).
66. Though the fallen angel is not mentioned explicitly in the creation account, it is widely accepted that the serpent in the garden is the same as the fallen angel mentioned elsewhere in the biblical narrative. This understanding is justified through several scriptural references: Rev. 12:9; Matt. 25:41; Is. 14:12–15.
67. Wheatley, "Thoughts on the Works of Providence," p. 15, line 10.
68. Wheatley, "To the University of Cambridge," pp. 15–16, lines 10–20.
69. Wheatley, "To the University of Cambridge," p. 15, lines 10–11.
70. Ironically, she positions the students above herself and her kind so that by the time she reaches the final three lines of the poem, she can subvert the position she initially establishes, suggesting a lower species/Ethiop/African, imbued with divine power, "tells you" (line 28) something that you were unaware of.
71. Wheatley, "On Whitefield," p. 23, line 30, 36.
72. Wheatley, "To the University of Cambridge," line 36 original.
73. Wheatley, "To the University of Cambridge," p. 15, line 13.
74. Lk. 23:34 (KJV).
75. Lk. 23:43 (KJV).
76. Wheatley, "To the University of Cambridge," p. 15, line 14.
77. 1 Sam. 16:7 (KJV).
78. Wheatley, "To the University of Cambridge," p. 15, line 17.
79. Wheatley, "To the University of Cambridge," p. 16, line 20.
80. Lk. 23:43 (KJV).
81. Balkun, "Phillis Wheatley's Construction of Otherness," 124.
82. Balkun, 125.
83. Balkun, 125.
84. Wheatley, "To the University of Cambridge," p. 16, line 18.
85. Wheatley, "To the University of Cambridge," p. 16, line 28.
86. Copeland, "Black, Hispanic/Latino, and Native American Theologies," 360.
87. Wheatley, "To the University of Cambridge," p. 16, line 24.
88. Chopp, "Latin American Liberation Theology," 413.
89. Phil. 2:5 (KJV).
90. Chopp, 413.
91. Wheatley, "To the University of Cambridge," p. 16, line 20.

Chapter 6

The Story behind the Voice

On Being Brought from Africa to America

> 'Twas mercy brought me from my *Pagan* land,
> Taught my benighted soul to understand
> That there's a God, that there's a *Saviour* too:
> Once I redemption neither sought nor knew.
> Some view our sable race with scornful eye,
> "Their colour is a diabolic die."
> Remember, *Christians*, *Negros*, black as *Cain*,
> May be refin'd, and join th' angelic train.[1]

With her poem, "On Being Brought from Africa to America," Wheatley sagaciously discusses redemption in a most sarcastic and transgressive manner. She uses satire throughout the poem. Though her readers at the time of publication did not fully comprehend the complexities of Wheatley's artistry, most scholars today note the reversal of roles and false adulations in these lines. In this poem, Wheatley presents the motif of redemption through spiritual transformation. Wheatley tells the reader, "'Twas mercy brought me from my *Pagan* land.'"[2] Wheatley's diction and style provide significant insight for understanding her motifs. She notes at the outset that "mercy" seems to be the catalyst for her physical freedom from her "pagan" homeland, leading to her salvation. A theological principle of protection, mercy typically describes God's sovereignty, particularly in matters of justice. Accordingly, Wheatley suggests it is God who delivers her from her "*Pagan* land" or sinful condition. Here, Wheatley implicitly sets up a dualism between her *Pagan* land and a non-Pagan land. She further delineates this dualism with terms like "benighted soul,"[3] "sable,"[4] and "diabolic."[5] In invoking this dualism, she repurposes negative descriptors of Africans and white people in the eighteenth century and questions the stable meanings of these terms. It is as likely as not, for example, that she understood Christianity's pagan roots. In this sense, the poem can be read as ironic.[6] If we accept this reading, we see that throughout the poem, she uses Eurocentric language to point out the corrupt (or at least coopted) nature of American Christianity. It seems, at first, that she only explicitly articulates one side of the dualism—darkness. The darkness, though, is representative of Christians' understanding of Paganism and of Christianity alike. Both could possess a benighted soul. Both are part of a sable race, one by birth and the other by deeds. Though Wheatley only explicitly deals with the darkness, through inference the reader can ascribe "light" or positive descriptors as Wheatley guides the reader through her refining experience, all the while masking her transgressive voice.

It is important to note as well that Wheatley further complicates notions of mercy in that she states "mercy . . . brought" her. The implication here is more complex than the traditional dichotomous view of either or pertaining to the meaning of concepts. She is not necessarily focusing primarily on her previous "*Pagan*" land or her new non-pagan land; rather, she could be dealing with the passage itself. As such, she is noting the events of the passage as much as the dichotomy between the two lands. Mercy serves as both catalyst and conveyor resulting in her experience of salvation. Through her pen, Wheatley marshals the reader through the passage of her becoming—a journey into the spiritual awareness and race-consciousness of the poet.

Will Harris suggests "Wheatley's distinctive response to the spirit of her times was to project a reflexively race-conscious presence in her poetry and personal letters" while maintaining her perception of blackness "as a western construction which blacks may simultaneously accept and trope according to contextual demands."[7] Significantly, Harris invokes the demonized other as a Eurocentric construction Wheatley seeks to recast. She "subverts the notion of an inherent evil in blackness by highlighting what for slave holders are the suppressed contradictions of divine grace and black intelligence."[8] Harris credits Wheatley's approach as echoing the Native American captivity narratives, which were "predominantly white-authored." This comparison is essential because the focus in each instance is on the white perception of the demonized other. Just as many of the captivity narratives are authored by white people, the perception of the African slave and her homeland as Pagan is "white-authored."

Because we know that Wheatley has some memory of Africa—she remembers her mother pouring water at the rising of the sun—we can assume that she has her own memory of her homeland and need not rely exclusively on white interpretations of it. John Shields's interpretation of Wheatley's memory of her mother pouring libations in her native "Pagan" land provides a good example of the complexity of reading Wheatley's memory. Shields writes: "Although such a ritual suggests the Islamic deity celebration of the dawn, it more directly points to the probability that Wheatley's parents were sun worshippers and helps to explain why in her slender body of poetry she alludes to Aurora eight times, Apollo seven, Phoebus twelve, and Sol twice."[9] As Harris and M'Baye note, Shields offers a compelling argument for an Islamic foundation for Wheatley, yet he insists on trivializing her parents' faith. The pouring of libations to welcome the dawning of a new day could be a reference to Wheatley's mother's adherence to one of the five pillars of Islam that is mandatory for salvation—performing the first of the five daily prayers. The early morning prayer, in this instance, would have been in reverence to God, with the sun being but one manifestation of God's presence. The pouring of water early in the morning, as Harris suggests, could also have been part of "the ritual washing Muslims are obligated to perform before each of the five daily prayers.... Wheatley may literally have meant pouring out water to cleanse oneself before prayer and before the sun has fully risen."[10] Harris ultimately concludes that Wheatley was probably aware of an African Muslim population within America who would potentially read her poetry. As such, he implies "Wheatley is coding . . . to a present and potentially literate African Muslim slave audience."[11] He continues, however, that this audience is "hypothetical" and that "Wheatley takes a potentially transgressive stance, for she appears to abandon the Muslim deity."[12] The reader will certainly note Wheatley's use of Christocentric notions throughout her poetry, but only the careful reader notices an Islamic presence among her engagement with common elements of Greek mythology. If anything, to use M'Baye's terminology, Wheatley successfully assumes "multiple identities" to present her plea for refinement and salvation.[13] Her invocation of Christ does not necessarily have to cancel out her Islamic faith; rather, her Islamic faith, as Abrahamic, enables her to expand her belief system to include tenets of Christianity. Both traditions believe in salvation, even if the method differs.

Howard Thurman recounts a conversation with a Hindu brother in 1935 in *Jesus and the Disinherited* that helps ground theoretically what Wheatley is doing:

> It was at a meeting in Ceylon that the whole crucial issue was pointed up to me in a way that I can never forget. . . . I was invited by the principal to have coffee. We drank our coffee in silence [then] he said to me, "What are you doing over here? I know what the newspapers say about a pilgrimage of friendship and the rest, but that is not my question. What are *you* doing over here? This is what I mean. . . . More than three hundred years ago your forefathers were taken from the western coast of Africa as slaves. The people who dealt in the slave traffic were Christians. One of your famous Christian hymn writers, Sir John Newton, made his money from the sale of slaves to the New World. He is the man who wrote 'How Sweet the Name of Jesus Sounds' and 'Amazing Grace'—there may be others, but these are the only ones I know. The name of one of the famous British slave vessels was 'Jesus.' The men who bought the slaves were Christians."[14]

He continued, "One of my students . . . sent me a clipping telling about a Christian church in which the regular Sunday worship was interrupted so that many could join a [lynch] mob. When [the man] had been [killed], they came back to resume [worshipping] their Christian God. I am a Hindu. I do not understand. Here you are in my country, standing deep within the Christian faith and tradition. . . . I am wondering what you, an intelligent man, can say in defense of your position."[15] Thurman notes that this is the mission of his prophetic witness—to justify his allegiance to the historical Jesus. Significant in his assertions is that the Jesus of the culture is a far cry from the Jesus of history. As he reiterates, the goal is to live into the representation of the historical Jesus, a representation that is lovecentric and liberative by nature. In concert across the annals of time with Thurman, Wheatley's invocation of Christ is a compliment to her African spiritual rootedness and, thereby, a deeper divine commitment to refine the soul of America, which has displaced the historical Jesus in favor of a compassionate Christ who is a complicit collaborator with evil in the guise of patriotism.

For Wheatley, the process of refining the soul of America and the individual involves the transformative process of salvation. Wheatley's use of "refining" alludes to the biblical notion of salvation. For example, Peter's first epistle suggests a direct correlation between trials and faith and the subsequent refinement/transformation that leads to salvation: "Wherein ye greatly rejoice, though now for a season, if need be, ye are in heaviness through manifold temptations: that the trial of your faith, being much more precious than of gold that perisheth, though it be tried with fire, might be found unto praise and honour and glory at the appearing of Jesus Christ."[16] Here, Peter compares an individual's faith to gold that has been transformed or refined through trials of fire. The process of refining involves transforming raw gold material into a precious, desirable, and valuable metal. The fire that refines gold can also destroy any impurities within the element. Alternately, the gold can become tarnished and ultimately perish because of negative reactions to oxygen that directly affects the traces of copper and silver within the refined gold.

Wheatley extends the analogy by applying it to pagans and Christians or darkness and light respectively. Accordingly, the individual soul can be tarnished by the external societal elements, or it can be refined into something precious. During the refining process, darkness must be consumed fully by the light to be transformed, or it will become tarnished if light is concealed. In this sense, Wheatley's appropriation of the refining process advocates that even those who have been converted to Christianity must be transformed before they can lay claim to salvation, "*Christians* . . . May be refin'd, and join th' angelic train."[17] Wheatley suggests a need for both light and darkness in the transformation process, an implicit extension of an argument for salvation for black people and white people. Despite being in different stages of salvific transformation, both the pagan and Christian are susceptible to darkness/sin and need to be refined.

Wheatley recognizes the universality of salvation and suggests that the practitioner of Christianity and the pagan can be tarnished without the refining process. Issuing a warning or reminder, she notes the dualism of Christian existence, the ever-present battle between light and darkness within America: "Remember, *Christians*, *Negros*, black as *Cain*, / May be refin'd, and join th' angelic train."[18] Ironically, the syntax here is ambiguous. It is not clear if the line includes items in a series or a direct address. If the latter is the case, we assume that Wheatley is speaking to Christians about Negroes. But the line could also be read to suggest the similarity between the Negroes and Christians. If both the Negroes and (presumably white) Christians are black as Cain (in terms of their sinfulness), the remedy of redemption or salvation is a transformative process that grants equal access to the "angelic train"—for example, the process of deliverance.

Wheatley's reference to Cain further supports her liberation theology by chronicling an episode of mercy that led to salvation and later freedom. Cain, typically used in Eurocentric thought to categorize the descendants of the African Diaspora, represents the son who was cast out of his native land and forced to roam as punishment for killing his brother Abel. However, Eurocentric thought also infrequently acknowledges that Cain was cast out of his homeland as an act of mercy, a form of protection from those who would have retaliated against him. His life is preserved, even as he is cast out of his homeland. Contrarily, Africans were forced out of their homeland as white people sought to expand their empire while many Europeans fled their homeland to escape religious persecution. Hence both groups were displaced, one because of greed and the other because of corrupt religious practices, yet both were potential beneficiaries of mercy and salvation.

Moreover, the reality is that Adam and Eve's son Seth was also born in the land of Cush (northern Africa) and had his children there. Seth's grandson Noah would then become the preserver of the nations through the flood. Hence, the descendants of Cain would have been wiped out in the flood. Africans, then, were not descendants of Cain; rather, they are most likely descendants of Ham. Still, the argument that the curse of Ham's son Canaan resulted in his blackness and thereby his servitude to his "white" relatives, the descendants of Shem and Japheth, is unfounded because Ham, Canaan, Shem, Japheth, and everyone within the biblical world of that time were black; they were African. As Theron Williams suggests, "Race was never an issue with the biblical writers. For them, there was only one race—the human race."[19] The assumption is that blacks make up a minority in the bible when the opposite is actually true. Of the major religions in the world, only Christianity has been completely whitewashed and Europeanized. The truth is that "no major religion was ever founded on the continent of Europe."[20] Race, then, emerges as the major identifier of those who are seeking to find and redefine themselves at the expense of using and displacing other people and other histories.

> Prior to American colonization, Europeans never identified themselves as the White race; they distinguished themselves according to nationality—Dutch, Scottish, English, Irish, Italian, and other European nationalities. It was not until the colonization of America that skin color, or race, became important. Race was made an issue for psychological, economic, political, religious and, later, social purposes.[21]

Williams's assertion that race is constructed for a selfish need to differentiate is significant. Wheatley's reading of the biblical narrative is undoubtedly informed by her history and knowledge of Europeans in America and on the continent of Europe. Perhaps she noticed a transatlantic difference in the approach to life in community. Cain (and many biblical characters for that matter) can be used as a symbolic representation for Wheatley. As she constructs her vision for a new America, she is keenly aware of the rewriting of people and places within and outside of the biblical narrative. For this reason, she further complicates the common understanding of who Cain is and represents.

An alternative reading of the European experience of salvation might further Wheatley's strategic subversion of traditional Christian understanding by portraying Europeans as well as Africans as Cain in the poem. In this context, Cain better describes European Americans who, having enslaved their fellow man, are sinful/tarnished but no less eligible for salvation in Wheatley's estimation, as an act of mercy, as is the case with Cain. This outlook promotes more than mere equality between the plights of European Americans and black people in America. Perhaps it suggests that European Americans fled to America as an act of mercy to escape religious persecution, yet they have allowed themselves to be tarnished by prejudices.

In such a reading, Wheatley could be inverting the understood notions of salvation. Note her suggestion that there is a God and Savior too. We can assume that she is intentional in alluding to the duality of God. Accordingly, she knows of the God of the Old Testament and God as savior as outlined in the New Testament. The Old Testament focuses on the curse of Cain by a punishing God, while the New Testament focuses on salvation for the sinner, which is only achieved through acceptance of Jesus Christ as redeemer. As an African who recognizes ancestors as intercessors, thereby eliminating the need for a "Saviour," the line could be read as her tongue-in-cheek assertion that she "neither sought nor knew" she needed a "Saviour" to be redeemed. In addition, her Islamic background would have understood salvation as available to her without a "Saviour."[22] As an African, she knew God's hand of mercy long before her arrival in America. But if redemption is necessary, it must be available to all. If Christians and Negroes are black as Cain, there is a need for the transformation of both. This dual understanding of redemption promotes two types of transformation, a new reality for Negroes and a new direction for white Christians, which serves as the essence of her salvation theory.

Refinement also encompasses "intellectual and cultural improvement."[23] Particularly, if cultural improvement is the goal of her suggested process of refinement, then refinement must commence within culture, meaning there must be a new understanding of what and who comprises culture. Wheatley voices a new definition of salvation that promotes cultural improvement. Through this poem, Wheatley seems to represent the ideal democratic American cultural outlook that recognizes, particularly in the last two lines, the equality of humanity. However, her recognition of human equality rather than racial disparity is problematic, for readers ignore cultural improvement as being a significant by-product of the refining process.

Seeking to place Wheatley within a larger literary tradition, critics like June Jordan minimize the cultural import of her liberation theology, which is her focus on refinement, concepts of paganism and Christianity, and the universality of the need for saving. Jordan notes Wheatley's use of terms like "benighted," "Pagan," and "refined" but considers these terms nonsense, adding, "Even her bizarre interpretation of slavery's theft of Black life as a merciful rescue should not bewilder anyone. These are regular kinds of iniquitous nonsense found in white literature, the literature that [Wheatley] assimilated, with no choice in the matter."[24] Defining Wheatley's use of language and poetic thrust as assimilation deflates her transgressive voice and abdicates her poetry as merely imitation. Though some scholars have moved on from accepting Jordan's interpretation as valid, it is important to engage these types of arguments for the sake of explicitly framing the Africentric as an act of theoretical re-creation. Jordan's position could be classified as a "misread,"[25] as James Levernier has suggested, that wrongfully removes Wheatley from the struggle for freedom. This typical view of "On Being Brought from Africa to America" erroneously maintains "that its author wholeheartedly endorsed the racist colonial opinion that bringing Africans to America for use as slaves was morally justifiable because it brought Christianity to souls that might otherwise have perished in hell."[26] Even as Levernier provides a different reading than Jordan, he too fails to see the potential use of satire in the poem. He notes that Wheatley uses puns to elucidate implicitly "the misery of . . . [the] slaves who worked in sugar *refineries* and *dye* plantations in the West Indies."[27] In so doing, salvation is deemphasized, which dismisses Wheatley's understanding of Christian doctrine and practice and ignores the potential reinterpretation of how salvation is understood during her time. He later notes, however, that

Wheatley uses religious commentary throughout the poem, but like Jordan, Levernier excludes salvation from the analysis, thereby rendering a reading of the poem without considering its theological significance. Wheatley establishes a need for salvation in this poem and expresses how this type of view of humanity frees the enslaved and enslaver alike. Her hermeneutic is one of kingdom principles and awareness that highlights the involvement of the divine in human affairs. This involvement, however, is not by imposition; rather, it is based upon relationship and desire to realize the kingdom on earth "as it is in heaven."[28]

Just as Jesus knew "the goals of religion . . . could never be worked out within the then-established order,"[29] Wheatley, too, operates from within the order to project her dream birthed out of her experience and acquired knowledge to project a new reality that is universally accessible. There is room for everyone in her established community—a community that focuses on the least, the last, and the left out. She is speaking for the people of the passage.

As Jesus read in the temple, Wheatley proclaims through her pen, "The Spirit of the Lord is upon me, because he hath anointed me to preach the gospel to the poor; he hath sent me to heal the brokenhearted, to preach deliverance to the captives, and recovering of sight to the blind, to set at liberty them that are bruised, To preach the acceptable year of the Lord."[30]

NOTES

1. Wheatley, "On Being Brought from Africa," in *Poems on Various Subjects*, p. 18, lines 1–8.
2. Wheatley, "On Being Brought from Africa," p. 18, line 1.
3. Wheatley, "On Being Brought from Africa," p. 18, line 2.
4. Wheatley, "On Being Brought from Africa," p. 18, line 5.
5. Wheatley, "On Being Brought from Africa," p. 18, line 6.
6. See Greg Carr and Dana A. Williams's "Toward the Theoretical Practice of Conceptual Liberation: Using an Africana Studies Approach to Reading African American Literary Texts" for a reading of Wheatley's use of irony in "On Being Brought from Africa to America." In Lovalerie King and Shirley Moody-Turner's *Contemporary African American Literature: The Living Canon* (Bloomington: Indiana University Press, 2013), 301–27.
7. Harris, "Diaspora Subjectivity," 36.
8. Harris, "Diaspora Subjectivity," 38.
9. Shields, "Phillis Wheatley's Use of Classicism," 103.
10. Harris, "Phillis Wheatley: A Muslim Connection," 4–5.
11. Harris, "A Muslim Connection," 6.
12. Harris, "A Muslim Connection," 6.
13. M'baye, *The Trickster Comes West*, 23.

14. Thurman, *Jesus and the Disinherited*, 13–14.
15. Thurman, 14–15.
16. 1 Pet. 1:6–7 (KJV).
17. Wheatley, "On Being Brought from Africa," p. 18, lines 7–8.
18. Wheatley, "On Being Brought from Africa," p. 18, line 7.
19. Williams, *The Bible Is Black History*, 38.
20. Williams, 105.
21. Williams, 108.
22. Harris, "A Muslim Connection," 3.
23. Davis, "Personal Elements," 194.
24. Jordan, "The Difficult Miracle," 255.
25. Levernier, "Style as Protest," 181.
26. Levernier, 181.
27. Levernier, 182.
28. Matt. 6:10 (KJV).
29. Thurman, 35.
30. Lk. 4:18–19 (KJV).

Epilogue
To Whom Much is Given

I must admit, this has been a journey. Not just the writing but the immersion experience as well. I have been immersed in the waters of eighteenth-century American identity formation. I'm sure there are stones that have been left unturned and arguments that do not live up to certain expectations. Perhaps that work will be done by the next person within the tradition. For any shortcomings or perceived failings with this project in my attempt to wrestle with this important and meaningful content, I simply say that I trust some scholar somewhere will reengage and enhance what is here. In the preceding pages, I have attempted to speak to the present moment of race relations in America through engagement with the various constructs of the nation's infancy and coming of age. For that matter, I am hopeful. Though it seems we haven't made much progress and, at times, the odds seem perpetually against those of us who have been kissed by the sun, I am hopeful. Not so much that this nation will, as the prodigal son in the bible, come to herself in an instant. Rather, I am hopeful that the continued agitation and stirring and troubling of the constructed waters of complacency and contra-divine, contra-communityisms will compel a renewed commitment to justice and equality. Reparations can happen but not without a radical rejection of "the way things were" and a needful negation of misplaced efforts to "make America great again." It is incumbent upon the scholar, preacher, and citizen to stand up and let the imaginative and creative expressions of the heart ring out to convict, correct, convince, and compel a lost people to be and do better. To me, this is living into the tradition marked out by Phillis Wheatley.

Through these poems, Wheatley articulates humanity's impatient principle and uses systematic theology, particularly soteriology and creation theories. Particularly, in "To the University of Cambridge" and "On Imagination," she expresses her awareness of the created order of things and the underlying principle that God is the ultimate creator of a just universe. Her articulation of a new creation within present reality is expressed in "To the Rev. Dr. Thomas Armory." In addition, in "To the University of Cambridge" Wheatley acknowledges her convictions for the redemption of corrupt humanity. The need for redemption is equally addressed in "On Being Brought from Africa to America" and "On the Death of Rev. Mr. George Whitefield." Here, Wheatley presents how salvation can be realized in all humanity, whether slave or free, black or white, American or African. Through "On the Works of Providence," "On Imagination," and "Hymn to Humanity," she exposes the common reality of human frailty and flawed-ness, building her argument for a new creation.

I must extend this invitation and plea once again: "Come into the water." As a reminder, this water is not necessarily your mother's or grandmother's water. This is not the waters of the Senegal River or Thames River. This is not the death chilling currents of the Atlantic or mighty Mississippi, yet it is infused with radicality and transformational insight. In a society wherein religion and race have determined the humaneness and social status of people, there is a need to reexamine its morals and politics. However, traditional approaches cannot be used to unearth the insidious ills that have thwart human compassion and maligned spirituality. Hence, a morally corrupt nation must be purged through immersion in this water to find the foundational principles for communal living. Ultimately, the plea for a new kind of baptism can produce an ethical rebirth in America while, as Charles Chesnutt's narrator suggests, "There's time enough, but none to spare."[1] Deliverance is both accessible and appropriate today, just as it was in the eighteenth century.

A reorientation within American culture to see and accept difference requires all people to have a renewed mind—to be immersed in the spiritual waters of morality—to view other human beings as equal. Phillis Wheatley presents compelling arguments for white people to radically engage in this renewal or new birth. Additionally, they present a call for black people to see themselves differently by re-presenting black people as trailblazers and as heroes and heroines overcoming insurmountable odds. The hope espoused by her pushes the committed scholar and common reader alike to engage in radical reform to tip the scales of racism and whiteness in America. The preferred method of reconciliation and reparations rests in renewed vision. As long as there are human beings living in community, there is an opportunity for mutual equality.

The focus of this book has been morality and ethics because it is the moral argument that has consistently been present throughout black writings and movements in America, and it is the moral agenda that will reclaim the spirit of this nation. As Richard S. Newman suggests, "Indeed, from Richard Allen and Prince Hall in the 1790s to David Walker and Maria Stewart in the late 1820s, African Americans developed an arsenal of strategies and tactics that diverged sharply from the learned and dispassionate legal/political activism of white abolitionists."[2] Black people "injected moralism and emotionalism" into racialized America hoping to inspire people to combat, at all costs, racism and discrimination of all kinds differently.[3] The "dispassionate" political approach would not suffice because politics aims to maintain the "right" or "just" façade while an immoral undercurrent erodes the community's social, economic, and spiritual foundation as well as its political systems.

Wheatley stands out amongst her contemporaries as they attempt to address, directly or indirectly, the hypocrisy within their distinctly American religious and political structures that affect the entire nation and not merely the black race. Like many of these authors, I argue change cannot occur within America unless the transformational message is accessible to black people and white people alike. During the era in which Wheatley and her contemporaries published, however, some of the transformational rhetoric was masked or presented in a coded manner, yet the call for an ethical rebirth permeates their works. I am speaking of writers like Douglass, Jacobs, Stewart, Walker, Cooper, Chesnutt, and Harper. Writing to uplift black people, they are bold enough to attack the root of the race issue: whiteness and the crippling effects of the (mis)appropriation of divine right. These writers espouse "a superior [moral] stance toward the American world" in hopes of presenting a rationale for individual change, leading to communal change.[4]

Immersion involves a (re)newed constitution and vision. Miroslav Volf suggests, upon the conversion of an individual or the renewal of the mind, the "Spirit does not erase bodily inscribed differences, but allows access into the one body of Christ to the people with such differences on the same terms."[5] Once the individual is transformed spiritually, at the seat of his or her morality, the possibility emerges for a new communal reality because "the Spirit [erases or at least loosens] . . . a stable and socially constructed correlation between differences and social roles."[6] The "othered" individual ceases to be the other socioeconomically and is grafted into the community as an equal.

I contend that it is necessary for all to understand the symbolic representation of Christ. I am not necessarily pushing for the acceptance of the historical Jesus as personal Lord and savior; however, I am advocating an acceptance of the principles for which Christ stood. The historical Jesus consistently broke down barriers and attempted to shift the cultural landscape. The Apostle Paul in Romans 12 asserts, "I beseech you therefore brethren, by the mercies of God, that ye present your bodies a living sacrifice, holy, acceptable unto God, which is your reasonable service. And be not conformed to this world: but be ye transformed by the renewing of your mind, that ye may prove what is that good, and acceptable, and perfect, will of God"[7] (v. 1–2). The renewal of the mind is necessary for the restoration of a unified humanity within America. My argument is that this is the ultimate call for humanity within community. It is true, all communities consist of several different types of people, from different walks of life, with different goals and strivings as well as spiritual orientation, yet as a foundational principle, the mind must be renewed in order to change the way "othered" people are viewed and acknowledged.

It is my desire that the same radical lens with which Wheatley views the American social constructs and creatively analyzes the American moral compass will be the lens with which scholars within the tradition also view and analyze America. Racism in America seems to be a cyclical phenomenon, and it is my suggestion that the way to eradicate this "fever" is to push for a moral revolution. Since our morality directly informs our ethical stance, an ethical revival is dependent upon a moral revolution. Langston Hughes articulates as much is his poem "Harlem," noting the severity of the "fever" that has stricken America:

> What happens to a dream deferred?
> Does it dry up
> like a raisin in the sun?
> Or fester like a sore—
> And then run?
> Does it stink like rotten meat?
> Or crust and sugar over—
> like a syrupy sweet?
> Maybe it just sags
> like a heavy load.
> *Or does it explode?*8

Dreams are prescriptively at the core of American life and mission, both individually and collectively. Yes, we are in pursuit of happiness, but life and liberty are guaranteed to serve as the seedbed for our dreams. When life is a given and liberty or freedom is assumed, dreams not only emerge, but become possible. Simply, dreams formulate into hopes and desires that, once effort and energy are applied, become a new reality. Hence, we arrive at a so-called American Dream, which is actually a reality, when life and liberty jettison a dream that is not blocked or encumbered by the very system that encourages it. The problem for black and brown sisters and brothers in America is that neither life nor liberty is guaranteed, so happiness remains a fallacy at worst and a forbidden fruit at best. Hughes approaches this concept of a deferred dream in a systematic and, arguably, clinical manner.

The poetic physician Hughes asks a series of investigatory subquestions in hopes to lead the nation to a successful cure to the principal ailment—racism, as manifested in the pervasiveness of deferred dreams for certain people. What if Dr. Hughes is diagnosing a white patient in his Harlem office? The same questions and potential consequences apply; however, the final question takes on new meaning. The question, "Or does it explode?," becomes a prescriptive plea for realignment. Sometimes bones literally have to be broken in order to reposition them for proper alignment. To put it another way, at times there is no real way to simply reform, revive, or restructure without an explosion. If happiness is defined and policed by the framers (who were white), and life and liberty are meant to be pursued by those considered a full part of the original people group with access to the American Dream, then there is a need for a major disrupting, dismantling, and deconstruction in order to reconstruct. That means that the prescription requires the dominant culture to choose to allow their deferred dream to explode. When it comes to deferring dreams, however, I continue to fight for access to control the outcome. It remains, though, that blacks in America have only a certain amount of control, particularly as it relates to the consequences of their involuntary deferral. It is ultimately a deferral of our personhood, humanity, and societal worth.

The foundation is laid; the examples are before us. The trajectory is hopeful, and the pump has been primed. Now, it is our turn to tip the scales of racism through our radical approach to scholarship. We must move beyond the comfortable space of theorizing to the uncomfortable and, at times, discomforting space of active engagement. So again, I conclude this book in a similar manner that I began. It was Rev. Dr. Martin Luther King Jr., in a speech entitled "The Vision of a World Made New," who suggests, "In every age men have quested and longed for a new order . . . [these persons see] justice conquering injustice, [these persons see] the forces of darkness consumed by the forces of light. Ultimately history brings into being the new order to blot out the tragic reign of the old order."[9] Are we willing to learn from history in our quest for a new order? Are we willing to see a new path and take it? Are we willing to agitate, agitate "for the struggle may be a moral one," to "suppress the deadly serpent in its egg" so [America] can be "wash'd in the fountain of Redeeming blood"?[10] There is certainly "time enough," for we are still here after all we have been through as a people. My question is: have we spent enough time wrestling with theories of race and racism in America? It seems to me that it is time to move beyond the page, beyond the library stacks, beyond the classroom and enter a new territory: the community. Phillis Wheatley worked and produced among her people and not in isolation. Perhaps this is our way forward.

"For unto whomsoever much is given, of him [or her] shall much be required."

Luke 12:48

NOTES

1. Chesnutt, *The Marrow of Tradition*, 195.

2. Newman, *The Transformation of American Abolitionism*, 87.
3. Newman, 87.
4. Bruce, *The Origins of African American Literature*, 83.
5. Volf, *Exclusion and Embrace*, 48.
6. Volf, 48.
7. Rom. 12:1–2 (KJV).
8. Hughes, "Harlem," in *The Collected Poems*, 426.
9. King, Martin Luther, Jr., "The Vision of a World Made New," 182–183.
10. Douglass, "West India Emancipation." Wheatley "To the University of Cambridge," p. 16, line 26; and "On Whitefield," p. 23, line 36.

Appendix 1

FURTHER READING

Baker, Houston. *Blues, Ideology, and Afro-American Literature: A Vernacular Theory*. Chicago: University of Chicago Press, 1984.

Bennett, Paula, "Phillis Wheatley's Vocation and the Paradox of the 'Afric Muse.'" *PMLA* 113, no.1 (January 1998): 64–76. http://doi.org/10.2307/463409.

Bloom, Harold, ed. *African American Poets: Volume 1; 1700s-1940s*. New York: Chelsea House Pub, 2009.

Brooks, Cleanth, and William Wimsatt. *Literary Criticism: A Short History*. New York: Vintage, 1967.

Bynum, Tara. "Phillis Wheatley on Friendship." *Legacy: A Journal of American Women Writers* 31, no. 1 (2014): 42–51. https://www.jstor.org/stable/10.5250/legacy.31.1.0042.

Bynum, Tara. "Phillis Wheatley's Pleasures: Reading Good Feeling in Phillis Wheatley's Poems and Letters." *Commonplace: The Journal of Early American Life* 11, no. 1 (October 2010). http://commonplace.online/article/phillis-wheatleys-pleasures/.

Bynum, Tara. Review of *Phillis Wheatley Chooses Freedom: History, Poetry, and the Ideals of the American Revolution*, by G. J. Barker-Benfield. *Journal of the Early Republic* 40, no. 3 (Fall 2020): 543–546. http://doi:10.1353/jer.2020.0068.

Cahill, Edward. *Liberty of the Imagination: Aesthetic Theory, Literary Form, and Politics in the Early United States*. Philadelphia: University of Pennsylvania Press, 2012.

Carter, J. Kameron. "Race, Religion and the Contradictions of Identity: A Theological Engagement with Douglass's 1845 Narrative." *Modern Theology* 21, no. 1 (January 2005): 37–65.

Carter, J. Kameron. *Race: A Theological Account*. Oxford: Oxford University Press, 2008.

Castronovo, Russ. "Something Else: The Politics of Early American Literature." *Early American Literature* 51, no. 2 (Special Issue 2016): 419–428.

Cone, James. *Black Theology and Black Power*. New York: Orbis Books, 1969.

Cone, James. *The Cross and the Lynching Tree*. New York: Orbis Books, 2011.

Cone, James. *God of the Oppressed*. New York: Orbis Books, 1975.

Cone, James. *Risks of Faith: The Emergence of a Black Theology of Liberation, 1968-1998.* Boston: Beacon Press, 1999.
Corbett-Hemeyer, Julia, ed. *Religion in America,* 7th ed. New York: Routledge, 2016.
Davis, Ron. "America's Early Bibles." International Society of Bible Collectors. First published Fall 2014 in *Bible Review Journal.* Updated 2021. http://www.biblecollectors.org/articles/early_american_bibles.htm.
Du Bois, W. E. B. "The Negro in Literature and Art." *The Annals of the American Academy of Political and Social Science* 49 (September 1913): 233–237. https://www.jstor.org/stable/1011924.
Franke, Astrid. "Phillis Wheatley, Melancholy Muse." *The New England Quarterly* 77, no. 2 (June 2004): 224–251. https://www.jstor.org/stable/1559745.
French, Scot A., and Edward L. Ayers. "The Strange Career of Thomas Jefferson: Race and Slavery in American Memory." In *Jeffersonian Legacies*, edited by Peter S. Onuf, 418–456. Charlottesville: University Press of Virginia, 1993.
Gates, Henry Louis, Jr. *The Trials of Phillis Wheatley: America's First Black Poet and Her Encounters with the Founding Fathers.* New York: Basic Civitas Books, 2003.
Glaude, Eddie S. *Democracy in Black: How Race Still Enslaves the American Soul.* New York: Crown, 2016.
Glaude, Eddie S. *Exodus! Religion, Race, and Nation in Early Nineteenth-Century Black America.* Chicago: University of Chicago Press, 2000.
Grant, Jacqueline. *White Women's Christ and Black Women's Jesus: Feminist Christology and Womanist Response.* Atlanta: Scholars Press. 1989.
Hatch, Nathan O. *The Democratization of American Christianity.* New Haven: Yale University Press, 1989.
Howell, William Huntting. *Against Self-Reliance: The Arts of Dependence in the Early United States.* Philadelphia: University of Pennsylvania Press, 2015.
King, Martin Luther, Jr. "Rediscovering Lost Values." In *The Papers of Martin Luther King, Jr.: Rediscovering Precious Values, July 1951-November 1955*, 248–256. Vol. 2. Berkeley: University of California Press, 1994.
Piersen, William D. *Black Yankees: The Development of an Afro-American Subculture in Eighteenth-century New England.* Amherst: University of Massachusetts Press, 1988.
Richmond, Merle A. *Bid the Vassal Soar: Interpretive Essays on the Life and Poetry of Phillis Wheatley and George Moses Horton.* Washington, DC: Howard University Press, 1974.
Robinson, William H. *Phillis Wheatley in the Black American Beginnings.* Detroit: Broadside Press, 1975.
Robinson, Willam H., ed. *Critical Essays on Phillis Wheatley.* Boston: G. K. Hall and Co., 1982.
Scheick, William J. "Phillis Wheatley's Appropriation of Isaiah." *Early American Literature* 27, no. 2 (1992): 135–140. https://www.jstor.org/stable/25056895.
Shields, John C. *Phillis Wheatley and the Romantics.* Knoxville: University of Tennessee Press, 2010.
Shields, John C. *Phillis Wheatley's Poetics of Liberation: Backgrounds and Contexts.* Knoxville: University of Tennessee Press, 2008.

Shields, John C., ed. *The Collected Works of Phillis Wheatley*. New York: Oxford University Press, 1988.

Sundquist, Eric J. *To Wake the Nations: Race in the Making of American Literature*. Cambridge, MA: Harvard University Press, 1993.

Bibliography

Allison, Gregg. *Historical Theology: An Introduction to Christian Doctrine.* Grand Rapids: Zondervan, 2011.
Armah, Ayi Kwei. *The Eloquence of the Scribes: A Memoir on the Sources and Resources of African Literature.* Popenguine, Senegal: Per Ankh, 2006.
Baker, Houston. *Journey Back: Issues in Black Literature and Criticism.* Chicago: University of Chicago Press, 1980.
Balkun, Mary McAleer. "Phillis Wheatley's Construction of Otherness and the Rhetoric of Performed Ideology." *African American Review* 36, no. 1 (Spring 2002): 121–135. http://doi.org/10.2307/2903370.
Bassard, Katherine Clay. *Spiritual Interrogations: Culture, Gender, and Community in Early African American Women's Writing.* Princeton: Princeton University Press, 1999.
Bercovitch, Sacvan. *The American Jeremiad.* Madison: University of Wisconsin Press, 2012.
Bernard, J. H., trans. Introduction and Notes to *Kant's Critique of Judgement*, by Immanuel Kant, 2nd rev. ed. London: Macmillan, 1914.
Bloch, Ernst. *Literary Essays.* Translated by Andrew Joron. Stanford: Stanford University Press, 1998.
Bloch, Ernst. *The Utopian Function of Art and Literature.* Translated by Jack Zipes and Frank Mecklenburg. Cambridge: MIT Press, 1989.
Bonhoeffer, Dietrich. *The Cost of Discipleship.* Translated by Reginald H. Fuller. New York: Macmillan, 1959.
Brake, Donald, and Shelley Beach. *A Visual History of the King James Bible.* Grand Rapids: Baker Books, 2011.
Bruce, Dickson D. *The Origins of African American Literature, 1680-1865.* Charlottesville: University of Virginia Press, 2001.
Brueggemann, Walter. *The Prophetic Imagination.* Minneapolis: Fortress Press, 2018.
Bushnell, Horace. "Pulpit Talent." In *The Company of Preachers: Wisdom on Preaching, Augustine to the Present*, edited by Richard Lischer, 83–89. Grand Rapids: William B. Eerdmans Publishing, 2002.

Cahill, Edward, and Edward Larkin. "Aesthetics, Feeling, and Form in Early American Literary Studies." *Early American Literature* 51, no. 2 (2016): 235–254. https://www.jstor.org/stable/43946747.

Carr, Greg, and Dana A. Williams. "Toward the Theoretical Practice of Conceptual Liberation: Using an Africana Studies Approach to Reading African American Literary Texts." In *Contemporary African American Literature: The Living Canon*, edited by Lovalerie King and Shirley Moody-Turner, 301–327. Bloomington: Indiana University Press, 2013.

Carter, J. Kameron. "Paratheological Blackness." *South Atlantic Quarterly* 112, no. 4 (Fall 2013): 589–611. https://doi.org/10.1215/00382876-2345189.

Castiglia, Christopher. "Revolution Is a Fiction: The Way We Read (Early American Literature) Now." *Early American Literature* 51, no. 2 (2016): 397–418. https://www.jstor.org/stable/43946747.

Chesnutt, Charles W. *The Marrow of Tradition*. New York: Norton, 2012. First published in 1901 by Houghton, Mifflin and Co. (Boston).

Chopp, Rebecca S. "Latin American Liberation Theology." In *The Modern Theologians: An Introduction to Christian Theology in the Twentieth Century*, edited by David F. Ford, 409–425. Hoboken, NJ: Blackwell Publishers, 1997.

Cone, James. "Theology's Great Sin: Silence in the Face of White Supremacy." In *The Cambridge Companion to Black Theology*, edited by Dwight N. Hopkins and Edward P. Antonio, 143–155. Cambridge: Cambridge University Press, 2012.

Cooper, Anna J. *The Voice of Anna Julia Cooper: Including a Voice from the South and Other Important Essays, Papers, and Letters*. Edited by Charles Lemert and Esme Bhan. Lanham, MD: Rowman & Littlefield, 1998.

Copeland, M. Shawn. "Black, Hispanic/Latino, and Native American Theologies." In *The Modern Theologians: An Introduction to Christian Theology in the Twentieth Century*, edited by David F. Ford, 357–388. Hoboken, NJ: Blackwell Publishers, 1997.

Cyrs, E. L. "The Ancient Craft of Jaliyaa." *Baba the Storyteller*. https://babathestoryteller.com/the-ancient-craft-of-jaliyaa/.

Davis, Arthur P. "Personal Elements in the Poetry of Phillis Wheatley." *Phylon* 14, no. 2 (2nd Quarter 1953): 191–198. http://doi.org/10.2307/271667.

Deleuze, Gilles, and Leopold von Sacher-Masoch. *Masochism: Coldness and Cruelty and Venus in Furs*. New York: Zone, 1991.

"Didn't My Lord Deliver Daniel?" In *The Norton Anthology of African American Literature*, Vol. 1, 3rd ed., edited by Henry Louis Gates Jr. and Valerie Smith, 17–18. New York: Norton, 2012.

Douglas, Kelly Brown. *Stand Your Ground: Black Bodies and the Justice of God*. New York: Orbis Books, 2015.

Douglass, Frederick. "West India Emancipation." Spoken by the author. August 3, 1857, Canandaigua, NY. Updated January 25, 2007. https://www.blackpast.org/.

Douglass, Frederick. "What to the Slave Is the Fourth of July?" In *The Oxford Frederick Douglass Reader*, edited by William L. Andrews, 108–130. New York: Oxford University Press, 1996.

Du Bois, W. E. B. *The Souls of Black Folk*. New York: Dover, 2007. First published in 1903 by A. C. McCurg & Co (Chicago).
Emerson, Ralph Waldo. "The Poet." In *The Harper Single Volume American Literature*, 3rd ed., edited by Donald McQuade, Robert Atwan, Martha Banta, Justin Kaplan, David Minter, and Robert Stepto, 554–568. New York: Addison-Wesley Educational Publishers, 1999.
Flanzbaum, Hilene. "Unprecedented Liberties: Re-Reading Phillis Wheatley." *MELUS* 18, no. 3 (Autumn 1993): 71–81. http://doi.org/10.2307/468067.
Forsyth, P. T. "The Authority of the Preacher." In *The Company of Preachers: Wisdom on Preaching, Augustine to the Present*, edited by Richard Lischer, 98–103. Grand Rapids: William B. Eerdmans Publishing, 2002.
"Go Down Moses." In *The Norton Anthology of African American Literature*, Vol. 1, 3rd ed., edited by Henry Louis Gates Jr. and Valerie Smith, 14–15. New York: Norton, 2012.
Greenslade, S. L., ed. *The Cambridge History of the Bible: The West from the Reformation to the Present Day*. Vol. 3. Cambridge: Cambridge University Press, 1963.
Grimsted, David. "Anglo American Racism and Phillis Wheatley's 'Sable Veil,' 'Length'ned Chain,' and 'Knitted Heart.'" *Women in the Age of the American Revolution*, edited by Ronald Hoffman and Peter J. Albert, 338–444. Charlottesville: University Press of Virginia, 1989.
Grudem, Wayne. *Systematic Theology: An Introduction to Biblical Doctrine*. Grand Rapids: Zondervan, 2000.
Guthrie, Nancy. *The Word of the Lord: Seeing Jesus in the Prophets*. Wheaton, IL: Crossway, 2014.
Hanson, Paul D. *Isaiah 40–66*. In *Interpretation: A Bible Commentary for Teaching and Preaching*, edited by James Luther Mays and Patrick D. Miller Jr. Louisville: Westminster John Knox Press, 1995.
Harris, Will. "Phillis Wheatley, Diaspora Subjectivity, and the African American Canon." *MELUS* 33, no. 3 (Fall 2008): 27–43. http://doi.org/10.1093/melus/33.3.27.
Harris, Will. "Phillis Wheatley: A Muslim Connection." *African American* 48, nos. 1–2 (Spring/Summer 2015): 1–15. http://doi.org/10.1353/afa.2015.0002.
Herbert, A. S. *Historical Catalogue of Printed Editions of the English Bible 1525-1961*. London: United Bible Societies, 1968.
Hills, Margaret T., ed. *The English Bible in America: A Bibliography of Editions of the Bible & New Testament Published in America, 1777-1957*. New York: Martino Fine Books, 1961.
The Holy Bible. King James Version, Zondervan, 1994.
Hubbard, Dolan. *The Sermon and the African American Literary Imagination*. Columbia: University of Missouri Press, 1996.
Hubbard, Dolan. "W.E.B. Du Bois and the Invention of the Sublime in *The Souls of Black Folk*." In *The Souls of Black Folk: One Hundred Years Later*, edited with an introduction by Dolan Hubbard, 298–321. Columbia: University of Missouri, 2003.
Hughes, Langston. "Harlem." In *The Collected Poems of Langston Hughes*, edited by Arnold Rampersad and David Roessel, 426. New York: Vintage, 1995.

Hughes, Langston. "The Negro Speaks of Rivers." In *The Collected Poems of Langston Hughes*, edited by Arnold Rampersad and David Roessel, 23. New York: Vintage Classics, 1994.

Jacobs, Harriet. *Incidents in the Life of a Slave Girl, Written by Herself*. In *Incidents in the Life of a Slave Girl, Written by Herself*, edited by Jean Fagan Yellin, 1–260. Cambridge, MA: The Belknap Press of Harvard University Press, 2009. First published in 1861 by Thayer and Eldridge (Boston).

Jefferson, Thomas. *Notes on the State of Virginia*. Edited by William Peden. Chapel Hill: University of North Carolina Press, 1982. https://www.jstor.org/stable/10.5149/9780807899809_jefferson.1.

Jordan, June. "The Difficult Miracle of Black Poetry in America or Something Like a Sonnet for Phillis Wheatley." *The Massachusetts Review* 27, no. 2 (Summer 1986): 252–262. https://www.jstor.org/stable/25089756.

Jusu, John, ed. *Africa Study Bible: NLT*. Carol Stream, IL: Tyndale House Publishers, 2017.

Kennedy, Rodney. "The Epistemic Power of Metaphor: A Rhetorical Model for Homiletics." PhD diss., Louisiana State University, 1990. *LSU Historical Dissertations and Theses*. 5063. https://digitalcommons.lsu.edu/gradschool_disstheses/5063.

King, Martin Luther, Jr. *Strength to Love*. New York: Pocket Books, 1964. https://archive.org/details/strengthtolove00king/page/n5/mode/2up.

King, Martin Luther, Jr. "The Vision of a World Made New." In *The Papers of Martin Luther King, Jr.: Advocate of the Social Gospel, September 1948-March 1963*, edited by Clayborne Carson et al., 181–184. Vol. 6. Berkeley: University of California Press, 2007.

Langley, April C. E. *The Black Aesthetic Unbound: Theorizing the Dilemma of Eighteenth-Century African American Literature*. Columbus: The Ohio State University Press, 2008.

Levernier, James A. "Style as Protest in the Poetry of Phillis Wheatley." *Style* 27, no. 2 (Summer 1993): 172–193. http://doi.org/ww.jstor.org/stable/42926037.

Levine, Lawrence W. *Black Culture and Black Consciousness: Afro-American Folk Thought from Slavery to Freedom*, Vol. 530. New York: Oxford University Press, 1977.

Lincoln, C. Eric. "The Development of Black Religion in America." In *African-American Religious Studies: An Interdisciplinary Anthology*, edited by Gayraud Wilmore, 5–21. Durham: Duke University Press, 1989.

Lischer, Richard. *The End of Words: The Language of Reconciliation in a Culture of Violence*. Grand Rapids: Eerdmans Publishing Company, 2005.

Long, Charles H. *Significations: Signs, Symbols, and Images in the Interpretation of Religion*. Philadelphia: Fortress, 1986.

Loscocco, Paula. *Phillis Wheatley's Miltonic Poetics*. London: Palgrave Macmillan, 2014.

M'Baye, Babacar. *The Trickster Comes West: Pan-African Influence in Early Black Diasporan Narratives*. Jackson: University Press of Mississippi, 2009.

Matson, R. Lynn. "Phillis Wheatley—Soul Sister?" *Phylon* 33, no. 3 (3rd Quarter 1972): 222–230. http://doi.org/:10.2307/273522.
Mays, James L. *Psalms*. In *Interpretation: A Bible Commentary for Teaching and Preaching*, Louisville: Westminster John Knox Press, 1995.
Mbiti, John S. *African Religions and Philosophy*, 2nd ed. Portsmouth, NH: Heinemann, 1969.
Miles, Margaret R. "Body Theology." In *The Westminster Dictionary of Christian Theology*, edited by Alan Richardson and John Bowden, 77. Louisville: Westminster Press, 1983.
Monescalchi, Michael. "Phillis Wheatley, Samuel Hopkins, and the Rise of Disinterested Benevolence." *Early American Literature* 54, no. 2 (2019): 413–444. http://doi:10.1353/eal.2019.0035.
Morrison, Toni. *What Moves at the Margin: Selected Nonfiction*. Jackson: University of Mississippi Press, 2008.
Nee, Watchman. *The Spiritual Man*. Bon Air, VA: Christian Fellowship Publishers, 1968.
Newman, Richard S. *The Transformation of American Abolitionism: Fighting Slavery in the Early Republic*. Chapel Hill: University of North Carolina Press, 2002.
Obama, Michelle. *Becoming*. New York: Crown, 2018.
Olney, James. "'I Was Born': Slave Narratives, Their Status as Autobiography and as Literature." *Callaloo*, no. 20 (1984): 46–73. http://doi.org/10.2307/2930678.
Otto, Rudolph. *The Idea of the Holy: An Inquiry into the Non-rational Factor in the Idea of the Divine and Its Relation to the Rational*. New York: Oxford University Press, 1923.
Paris, Peter. *The Social Teaching of the Black Churches*. Minneapolis: Fortress Press, 1985.
Prothero, Stephen. *American Jesus: How the Son of God Became a National Icon*. New York: Farrar, Straus, and Giroux, 2003.
Roberts, Wendy Raphael. *Awakening Verse: The Poetics of Early American Evangelicalism*. Cambridge, MA: Oxford University Press, 2020.
Rose, Matthew F. "Karl Barth's Failure: Matthew Rose Shows That Karl Barth Failed to Liberate Theology from Modernity's Captivity." *First Things: A Monthly Journal of Religion and Public Life*, no. 244 (June/July 2014): 39–44. https://link.gale.com/apps/doc/A368281511/EAIM?u=rock77357&sid=summon&xid=83a00475.
Sanders, E. P. *Historical Figure of Jesus*. New York: Penguin Books, 1993.
Scheick, William J. "Subjection and Prophecy in Phillis Wheatley's Verse Paraphrases of Scripture." *College Literature* 22, no. 3 (October 1995): 122–130. https://www.jstor.org/stable/25112212.
Shields, John C. "Phillis Wheatley's Use of Classicism." *American Literature* 52, no. 1 (March 1980): 97–111. http://doi.org/10.2307/2925190.
Spillers, Hortense Jeanette. "Fabrics of History: Essays on the Black Sermon." PhD diss., Brandeis University, 1974. ProQuest (7428017).
Stone, Howard W., and James O. Duke. *How to Think Theologically*, 3rd ed. Minneapolis: Fortress Press, 2013.

Taylor, Gardner C. *How Shall They Preach*. Elgin, IL: Progressive Baptist Publishing House, 1977.
Thurman, Howard. *Jesus and the Disinherited*. Boston: Beacon Press, 1976.
Tillich, Paul. *Theology of Culture*. Oxford: Oxford University Press, 1959.
Tomkins, Jane. *Sensational Designs: The Cultural Work of American Fiction, 1790-1860*. New York: Oxford University Press, 1985.
Volf, Miroslav. *Exclusion and Embrace: A Theological Exploration of Identity, Otherness, and Reconciliation*. Nashville: Abingdon Press, 2010.
Wesley, Charles, and John Wesley. "Hymn for Christmas-Day." In *Hymns and Sacred Poems*. London: Strahan, 1739.
West, Elizabeth J. *African Spirituality in Black Women's Fiction: Troubled Visions of Memory, Community, Nature, and Being*. Lanham, MD: Lexington Books, 2011.
Wheatley, Phillis. *The Poems of Phillis Wheatley*, edited with an introduction by Julian Mason Jr. Chapel Hill: University of North Carolina Press, 1966.
Wheatley, Phillis. *Poems on Various Subjects, Religious and Moral*. London: Forgotten Books, 2012. First published in 1773 by A. Bell (London).
Williams, Theron. *The Bible Is Black History*. Scotts Valley, CA: CreateSpace Independent Publishing Platform, 2018.
Wright, Richard. Introduction to *Black Metropolis: A Study of Negro Life in a Northern City*, edited by St. Clair Drake and Horace R. Cayton, lix–lxxvi. Chicago: University of Chicago Press, 1945.

Index

Advent, 37
aesthetics, 5;
   critique of, 6;
   and sublime, 49–52, 57n20
African culture:
   and benevolence, 24–25;
   Bible and, 110–11;
   and holism, 50;
   and spoken word, 46–47;
   and sun, 67, 75n17;
   and virtue, 73;
   Wheatley and, 9–10, 71, 96, 107, 112
Alan of Lille, 26
Allen, Richard, 118
alternative visions, 11–13;
   Du Bois and, 49;
   preaching and, 27;
   Wheatley and, 65, 94
American culture, 3;
   Douglass and, 23;
   Jeremiad in, 74;
   and Jesus, 48;
   and racism, 26–27;
   recommendations for, 118, 121;
   Wheatley and, 2, 5, 77–102, 113
American Dream, 120;
   versus history, 27;
   Wheatley and, 82
Amory, Thomas, 33–36

apocalypse, 70
Aristotle, 25
Armah, Ayi Kwei, 9, 46–47, 57n7, 72–73
art/artist, Wheatley and, 63–64, 69
atonement, 97

Baker, Houston, 19
Balkun, Mary McAleer, 100
Baraka, Amiri, 5
Barth, Karl, 4
Bassard, Katherine Clay, 9–10
becoming:
   Obama and, 29;
   Wheatley and, 108
benevolence, Wheatley and, 24–25
Bercovitch, Sacvan, 74
Bible, 1, 20–21;
   Genesis 1:26–2:7, 3, 64, 101;
   Genesis 2:17, 94;
   Genesis 3:4–5, 94;
   Deuteronomy 28:13, 22;
   Psalms 119:71, 71;
   Psalms 137, 23;
   Isaiah 6:5, 82;
   Isaiah 14:12–15, 105n66;
   Isaiah 63:1–8, 45–56;
   Jeremiah 18:3b-4, 35;
   Matthew 22:36–40, 55;

Matthew 23:1–12, 54–55;
Matthew 25:41, 105n66;
Luke 2:8–21, 103n24;
Luke 2:49, 39;
Luke 4:18–19, 114;
Luke 12:48, 14, 121;
Luke 23:34, 99;
Luke 23:43, 99;
John 1:1, 47, 64;
John 1:3, 64;
John 1:14, 47;
John 3:16, 38, 80;
John 8:36, 80;
John 19:28–34, 39;
Romans 12:1–2, 119;
Phillippians 2:1–11, 61–62, 72, 102;
1 Thessalonians 5:23, 3;
1 Peter 1:6–7, 110;
1 Peter 2:9a, 16n40;
Revelation 12:9, 105n66;
Revelation 21, 70–71
Black aesthetic, 5–6, 9
black body, 7–8, 11;
   Hughes and, 27;
   Wheatley and, 22
black liberation theology,
   development of, 4–5
blackness, Wheatley and, 9–10, 85–86
black people:
   and morality, 118–19;
   recommendations for, 118
black writers:
   on freedom, 11;
   on rebirth, 3
Bloch, Ernst, 6, 19
blood, Wheatley and, 39–41, 98
body theology, 7–8, 12
Bonhoeffer, Dietrich, 12, 16n41
born again. *See* rebirth
Brake, Donald, 1
Brawley, Benjamin, 65
Brown, Sterling A., 65
Brueggemann, Walter, 17–19

Cahill, Edward, 5–6, 49–50

Cain narrative, Wheatley and, 37, 111
Calvinism, 12, 42n11;
   and divine right, 2;
   and providence, 81;
   Wheatley and, 38, 84
Cambridge students, Wheatley
   and, 93–102
Carter, J. Kameron, 27, 31n48
Castiglia, Christopher, 5–6
catharsis, preaching and, 21
chaos:
   of history, Hubbard and, 20;
   Wheatley and, 88–91
cheap grace, 12–13, 16n41
Chesnutt, Charles, 13, 15n8, 118–19
church:
   and academy, 1;
   and exclusion, 12;
   and racism, 26–27
classical culture, Wheatley and, 34,
   67, 81, 107
colonization, and race, 112
commitment, Wheatley and, 72, 92
community:
   alternative possibilities for, 13;
   preaching and, 21;
   recommendations for, 117–19;
   Wheatley and, 71, 99
Cone, James, 1, 4–5, 26
conversion, 116–17
Cooper, Anna Julia, 9, 15n8, 119
creation, 29;
   Amory and, 34;
   biblical account of, 3, 92;
   imagination and, 61–62;
   Johnson and, 59, 72n3;
   Wheatley and, 57–73, 81,
   84–86, 92–95, 97
crucifixion, Wheatley and, 96–97
Crummell, Alexander, 4
culture:
   Tillich and, 30n2.
   See also American culture
curiosity:
   and poetry, 25;

Index

Wheatley and, 2, 18–19

darkness:
  Hubbard and, 20;
  Wheatley and, 85, 110–111
Davis, Arthur P., 40–41, 65
Descartes, René, 4, 72
descent, and re-creation, 70–71
"Didn't My Lord Deliver Daniel"
  (spiritual), 92
divine right, 3–4, 12, 119;
  and black body, 8;
  critiques of, 14;
  Wheatley and, 81–82, 95
double consciousness, 9
Douglas, Kelly Brown, 7–8
Douglass, Frederick, 13, 15n8, 23, 55, 119
dualism, Wheatley and, 40, 111
Du Bois, W. E. B., 4–5, 9, 15n8, 49–52
Duke, James, 17

earth, Wheatley and, 67
Eden, Wheatley and, 95–96
Edwards, Jonathan, 42n11
Elect, 12, 42n11, 81;
  Wheatley and, 38
Eliot, T. S., 30n8
Emancipation Proclamation, 2
Emerson, Ralph Waldo, 21, 85
encyclicals, 95
enlargement, and re-creation, 70–72
Enlightenment thought, 98;
  Wheatley and, 1–2
equality:
  alternative standard for, 11;
  Jesus and, 119;
  Wheatley and, 2, 95, 101, 113
ethics, 118;
  Wheatley and, 113.
  See also morality; rebirth, ethical
Ethiop, Wheatley and, 8
European culture:
  Wheatley and, 71, 107–8.
  See also classical culture

Evans, Joseph Norman, 4
evil, Wheatley and, 95
exaltation, 63–64;
  Wheatley and, 74
exclusion:
  Jefferson and, 11;
  Puritans and, 12
expression, 52

fallen man image, 27, 31n48
fancy, Wheatley and, 88
fidelity of God, Wheatley and, 87, 89
fire, Wheatley and, 72
First Amendment, 10
Flanzbaum, Hilene, 65
flood, 70, 72
force, and liberation, 81
Forsyth, P. T., 28
freedom, 10–11;
  Amory and, 34;
  preaching and, 20, 22;
  Second Amendment and, 10.
  See also liberation
free will, 28
Frelinghuysen, Jacob, 42n11
friendship, Wheatley and, 74

Gayle, Addison, 5
glorification of God, 104n24;
  Wheatley and, 84
God:
  fidelity of, 87, 89;
  image of, 29, 34;
  imagination and, 64;
  nature of, 5;
  Wheatley and, 34, 66–67, 77–93
"Go Down Moses" (spiritual), 91–92
grace:
  cheap, 12–13, 16n41;
  Wheatley and, 37–39, 100
Greek culture. *See* classical culture
Greenslade, S. L., 1
griots, 47, 57n3, 57n7;
  Wheatley as, 9, 47, 54
Grudem, Wayne, 105n65

Hall, Prince, 116
"Hark! The Herald Angels Sing" (Wesley), 65–66
Harper, Frances E. W., 15n8, 119
Harris, Will, 40–41, 96, 106–7
hate, Wheatley and, 85–86
Hegel, G. W. F., 4
Herbert, A. S., 1
hermeneutics, 10, 50
Hills, Margaret T., 1
history:
    versus American Dream, 27;
    Barth and, 4;
    Hubbard and, 20;
    Hughes and, 27–28
Homer, 34
homoousias, 54, 58n36
hope, 117, 119;
    griots and, 47
Hopkins, Samuel, 24–25
Hubbard, Dolan, 19–20, 27, 29, 49–52, 57n20
Hughes, Langston, 27–28, 120
humanity:
    and God, 5;
    Wheatley and, 2, 35, 60–61, 66–74, 95, 101
human nature, Bible and, 3
Hume, David, 4
humility, Alan of Lille and, 26
hymn, term, 67
"An Hymn to Humanity" (Wheatley), 60–61, 67–74, 118

identity politics, 6–8;
    Wheatley and, 42n11, 56
image of God, 29;
    Wheatley and, 34
imagination:
    African American, 19–20;
    Castiglia and, 6;
    and creation, 63–64;
    and God, 64;
    and liberation, 101;
    and theology, 17–20;
    Wheatley and, 59–66
incarnation, 7;
    Wesley and, 67–68
inclusion, Wheatley and, 11, 110–11
inequality, Wheatley and, 73
infusion, and re-creation, 70, 72
inspiration:
    poet and, 21–22, 25–26, 29;
    and re-creation, 70–71;
    Wheatley and, 47, 67, 82–83
interjection, sermon as, 29
inversion, Wheatley and, 22, 110
"Isaiah LXIII. 1–9" (Wheatley), 45–56
Islam:
    and scripture, 47;
    Wheatley and, 109
"I was born" opening, 7

Jacobs, Harriet, 55, 85, 119
jalimuso. See griots
Jefferson, Thomas, 8, 11, 49–50
Jehovah, 85, 89, 104n25.
    See also God
Jesus, 54–55;
    American culture and, 48;
    and liberation, 81;
    Paul and, 62;
    principles of, 119;
    Thurman and, 110;
    Wheatley and, 47, 52–53, 64–67, 70, 97
Johnson, James Weldon, 62, 65, 75n3
Jordan, June, 113
justice:
    Africanist culture and, 73;
    alternative standard for, 11
justification:
    alternative possibilities for, 13;
    Wheatley and, 36

Kant, Immanuel, 4, 50–51
Kennedy, Rodney, 88
King, Martin Luther, Jr., 20, 121
King James Version, 1
knowledge:

and power, 52;
  Wheatley and, 94, 95–96

Langley, April C. E., 5–6, 9
language:
  enslaved people and, 19;
  Wheatley and, 18–19, 81
Larkin, Edward, 5–6, 47–48
Latin, Wheatley and, 18, 83
Levernier, James, 34, 96, 113–14
Levine, Lawrence, 22
liberation:
  and imagination, 102;
  Wheatley and, 25, 35, 61, 81–93.
  See also freedom
liberation theology, 11–12;
  development of, 15n8;
  imagination and, 20;
  nineteenth century, 3–4;
  Wheatley and, 1–16
light, Wheatley and, 88–90, 110–11
Lincoln, Abraham, 2
Lincoln, C. Eric, 12
Lischer, Richard, 18, 21
literature:
  and prophetic voice, 10;
  and theology, 1
Liza, 84
Loggins, Vernon, 65
Long, Charles H., 30
Longinus, Cassius, 50–51
love, Wheatley and, 81–83, 87, 89–90

Maât, 9, 73
Manifest Destiny, 2;
  Wheatley and, 82
Mary of Nazareth, 103n17, 103n24
Matson, R. Lynn, 40–41, 96, 97
M'Baye, Babacar, 109
Mbiti, John S., 66, 75n17
meaning, African Americans and, 30
mercy, Wheatley and, 100, 107, 108, 112
metaphor:
  of fallen man, 27, 31n48;
  nature of, 88
Methodism, 68
Miles, Margaret, 7
mind:
  Paul and,102;
  renewal of, 118–20;
  Wheatley and, 56, 62, 64, 82
Monescalchi, Michael, 24–25
morality, 118;
  black people and, 118–19;
  and critique of white supremacy, 26;
  and slavery, 3;
  Wheatley and, 34, 54, 56
Morrison, Toni, 9, 15n34
muse, Wheatley and, 47, 69, 82–83

national identity, alternative standard for, 11
Native Americans captivity narratives, 108
nature:
  redemption and, 69;
  Wheatley and, 88, 94
Neal, Larry, 5
Nee, Watchman, 3
neoclassical approach, Wheatley and, 5
Newman, Richard S., 118–19
night, Wheatley and, 88, 90
not-yet-real, Bloch and, 6, 19

Obama, Michelle, 29
obedience unto death, preaching and, 63
Olney, James, 7
"On Being Brought from Africa to America" (Wheatley), 22, 34, 39, 107–14, 118;
  scholarship on, 107–8, 113
"On Imagination" (Wheatley), 22, 59–60, 117–18
"On the Death of the Reverend Mr. George Whitefield" (Wheatley), 8, 36–37, 118;
  scholarship on, 40–41
oral culture, 21;
  and preaching, 20, 28

Orunmila, 84
Otto, Rudolph, 50

paganism, Wheatley and, 70, 108
Paris, Peter, 26–27
passion, Wheatley and, 83
peace, Wheatley and, 84, 87
Pentecost, 37
perseverance, Wheatley and, 92
personhood, 6–8;
    alternative possibilities for, 13;
    Wheatley and, 19, 22, 25
Peters, John, 14n1
Poems on Various Subjects Religious and Moral (Wheatley), 5, 10
poet-preacher:
    nature of, 28–29;
    Wheatley as, 17–32
poetry, 2;
    Emerson and, 85;
    imagination and, 6, 19;
    and preaching, 21–22;
    and theology, 17–18;
    Wheatley and, 17–32, 64
politics, and theology, 24
power:
    and knowledge, 52;
    Wheatley and, 90
praise songs:
    Mary and, 103n17;
    Wheatley and, 83, 88, 91
preaching, 2, 20–22;
    and fallen man metaphor, 27, 31n48;
    and imagination, 20;
    nature of, 26;
    and obedience unto death, 63;
    poetry and, 21–22;
    Wheatley and, 1–2;
    versus written sermon, 20
press, freedom of, 10
privilege, Wheatley and, 95
prophetic voice, 6;
    and imagination, 17–18;
    Isaiah and, 47–48;
    Wheatley and, 10–11, 55, 99, 117–21

Prothero, Stephen, 48
providence, Wheatley and, 77–80
Puritanism, 12, 100

Ra, 84
race issues:
    Bible and, 111–12;
    recommendations for, 117–21;
    Wheatley and, 85, 118
racism:
    America and, 26–27;
    Jefferson and, 11
reason, Wheatley and, 81–82, 89–91
reasoned art, term, 49–50, 57n20
rebirth, ethical:
    black writers and, 3;
    nature of, 2–4;
    recommendations for, 118–19;
    Wheatley and, 2, 99–100, 114;
    Whitefield and, 38
re-creation, Wheatley and, 66–74;
    actions of, 70–73
redemption, Wheatley and, 65–74, 107, 117–18
refining, Wheatley and, 110, 113
reflexivity, creation and, Wheatley and, 62–66
refuge, Wheatley and, 53, 56
religion:
    freedom of, 10;
    Tillich and, 30n2
resilience, Wheatley and, 47, 53, 56
resistance, Wheatley and, 47, 53, 56
revivalism:
    Calvinism and, 42n11;
    Wheatley and, 8, 84
Revolutionary period, Wheatley and, 5
Roberts, Wendy Raphael, 7–8
Roman culture. *See* classical culture
Rose, Matthew, 4

salvation:
    griots and, 47;
    Wheatley and, 35–40, 52–53, 77–102
Sanders, E. P., 48

Sankofa bird, 47, 57n7
satire, Wheatley and, 113
Scheick, William J., 1–2
scholarship:
   on Biblical translations, 1;
   on Black aesthetic, 5;
   on "Cambridge," 94, 97;
   on eighteenth century
      Aesthetics, 5–6;
   on identity politics, 7;
   on "On Being Brought from Africa,"
      107–8, 113–14;
   on "On the Death of Rev. Mr. George
      Whitefield," 40–41;
   recommendations for, 117–
      18, 120–21;
   on Wheatley and race, 65–66
science, Wheatley and, 97–98
self-empowerment, 12
self-worth, ontological, 6–8
Senegambian poetics, 9
seraphim, 83
serpent, 102n66;
   Wheatley and, 94, 95, 97
Sewall, Joseph, 34
Shields, John, 108–9
silence, poet and, 18
sin, 81, 105n65;
   slavery and, 26–27;
   Wheatley and, 38–39, 94–97, 99
slavery/slavocracy:
   Baker on, 19;
   Hopkins and, 25;
   liberation theology and, 11–12;
   and soul, 3;
   Wheatley and, 24–25, 54–56, 96–102
slave trade, and black body, 7–8
soteriology:
   Eurocentric, 12–13;
   Wheatley and, 38, 69
soul:
   nature of, 3;
   Wheatley and, 83
speech, freedom of, 10
Spillers, Hortense, 21, 27, 31n48

spirit, nature of, 3
spoken word, 46
Stewart, Maria, 13, 15n8, 118–19
Stone, Howard, 17
Stuckey, Sterling, 19
sublime, 55n20;
   Aesthetics and, 49–52
submission, Wheatley and, 72
sun:
   Africanist culture and, 67, 75n17;
   Wheatley and, 67, 83–84, 87, 90, 108
support, and re-creation, 70–71

Tennent, Gilbert, 42n11
theology:
   black, 11–12;
   and literature, 1;
   and politics, 24;
   practice of, 17;
   and prophetic voice, 10;
   Wheatley and, 1–2, 17–32,
      83–85, 117.
   See also liberation theology
thirsty, Wheatley and, 38–39
"Thoughts on the Works of Providence"
   (Wheatley), 77–102
Thurman, Howard, 109–10
Tillich, Paul, 30n2
"To Maecenas" (Wheatley), 34
Tomkins, Jane, 6
"To the Rev. Dr. Thomas Amory . . . "
   (Wheatley), 33–36, 117
"To the University of Cambridge,
   in New-England" (Wheatley),
   93–102, 117–18;
   scholarship on, 98, 99, 100
transformation, Wheatley and, 2, 35–38
Trinity, Wheatley and, 90
trust, preaching and, 28

Ubuntu, 25
universalism, Wheatley and,
   63–64, 111, 113
Utu, 84

veil, Wheatley and, 87–88
vices:
   term, 53;
   Wheatley and, 97
virtue, Wheatley and, 73
voice:
   of poet-preacher, 29–30;
   prophetic, 10–11
Volf, Miroslav, 119

Walker, David, 13, 15n8, 118–19
Wesleyan thought, 42n11, 67–68
West, Elizabeth J., 66
"What to the Slave is the Fourth of July?" (Douglass), 23
Wheatley, John, 2, 18
Wheatley, Phillis:
   classification of, 13;
   education of, 2, 18–19;
   influences on, 33–42;
   and liberation theology, 1–16;
   life of, 105–13;
   as poet-theologian, 17–32;
   as prophetic poet, 10–11, 54, 56, 94
White, Hayden, 20
Whitefield, George, 8, 34, 36–40, 42n11, 67–68
white people:
   progressive salvation and, 99;
   recommendations for, 118
white supremacy, 26;
   Wheatley and, 86–87.
   See also slavery/slavocracy
Williams, Theron, 111–12
winepress, Wheatley and, 52–53
wisdom, Wheatley and, 84, 90
works righteousness, 13, 42n11;
worth righteousness, 13, 16n42
wretched, Wheatley and, 39
Wright, Richard, 65
writing:
   importance of, 20–21;
   Wheatley and, 18

About the Author

Reverend **Wallis C. Baxter III**, PhD, serves as the senior pastor of the Second Baptist Church Southwest in District Heights, Maryland. He is an adjunct professor of African American Literature at Gettysburg College and an academic research fellow at the Benjamin L. Hooks Institute for Social Change at the University of Memphis. Currently, he is coediting a series of sermons delivered during the COVID-19 pandemic.

www.ingramcontent.com/pod-product-compliance
Lightning Source LLC
Chambersburg PA
CBHW020126010526
44115CB00008B/988